THE MEXICAN CINEMA

DATE DUE			
Mar 15 '82			
'82			

THE MEXICAN CINEMA
Interviews with Thirteen Directors

by Beatriz Reyes Nevares

Introduction by E. Bradford Burns

Translators: Elizabeth Gard and Carl J. Mora

UNIVERSITY OF NEW MEXICO PRESS   **Albuquerque**

Library of Congress Cataloging in Publication Data

Reyes Nevares, Beatriz.
  The Mexican cinema: Interviews with Thirteen Directors

  Translation of Trece directores del cine mexicano.
  Bibliography: p. 171
  Includes index.
  1. Moving-picture producers and directors—
Mexico—Interviews. I. Title.
PN1998.A2R4913   791.43'0232'0922 [B] 75-40835
ISBN 0-8263-0410-9
ISBN 0-8263-0411-7 pbk.

English translation of Preface, Author's Introduction, Chapters 1–6 © 1976 by
  Carl J. Mora. All rights reserved
English translation of Chapters 7–13 © 1976 by Elizabeth Gard. All rights
  reserved
Introduction © 1976 by E. Bradford Burns. All rights reserved
Manufactured in the United States of America
Library of Congress Catalog Card Number 75–40835
International Standard Book Number (clothbound) 0–8263–0410–9
International Standard Book Number (paperback) 0–8263–0411–7
First Edition
Originally published as *Trece directores del cine mexicano* © 1974 by
Secretaría de Educación Pública, SEP/SETENTAS, Sur 124, núm. 3006, México 13,
  D.F., México

With my gratitude to Lic. Alejandro Carrillo M.

Contents

Foreword

Caught between economic imperatives and creativity's complex demands, the cinema has ceased to be a simple esthetic activity and become the most sensitive barometer of contemporary society. As a result the cineasts find themselves trapped by this dilemma, beneath which lies the critical conscience of the industrial age.

The force of events has succeeded only in overwhelming them; weary of compromise, orphans of estheticism, they have been obliged to flee from simple stylistic expression toward a seizure of conscience. This process, which has caused dislocations unknown to practitioners of the other arts, is splendidly discussed in this book. Beatriz Reyes Nevares has succeeded in capturing and scrutinizing the essence of thirteen distinguished Mexican cineasts.

Midway between scholarship and criticism, her survey becomes a unique analysis, impartially contemplating both the history of a disquieting activity and the first signs of a marvelous achievement. The minute the cameras stop, the directors become introspective, parenthesizing their own personalities, and deliver themselves into one of the most complex and risky of psychological exercises—self-criticism. The principal merit of this book lies in its stealthy approach to the sanctuary of self-awareness so as to bring it into the light of day and expose it to open view. Imagination confronts itself: while gazing at the depths of their own secrets, the cineasts open the door to discussion and establish the premises of the dialogue. By faithfully accompanying them in this singular adventure, this book becomes more than a mere survey and reaches for the pinnacles of creativity. A critique of a critique. A critique of the imagination. A critique, finally, of silence and its consequences.

Rodolfo Echeverría Alvarez

Introduction

Movies have a long and fascinating history in Latin America. They made a very early appearance in that part of the world. Within months after the Lumière brothers astonished the Parisians with their flickering films, several Latin American capitals boasted their own movie houses which curious crowds filled. Not long thereafter pioneer filmmakers in Latin America began to record their surroundings on celluloid with their newly imported, cumbersome cameras.

In Mexico, the first public cinema spectacle took place on August 21, 1896, only eight months later than in Paris. The number of movie houses multiplied rapidly thereafter so that by 1900 they could be found in all parts of the republic. In conformity with the dominant Positivist ideology of that era in Mexico, the early filmmakers sought to capture "reality" with their cameras. The first films recorded the daily life of the capital. Much filmic attention focused on the omnipotent president, Porfirio Díaz, seemingly a permanent resident of the presidential palace after 1876. The early, primitive one-reelers included a large number of titles such as *Viaje del General Díaz a Puebla, Las fiestas presidenciales en Yucatán,* or *El General Porfirio Díaz a caballo por Chapultepec.* (The last one remained on the capital screens for more than a year!)

From recording the present, the early Mexican filmmakers moved to a filmic reconstruction of the past. The approaching centennial—in 1910 Mexico celebrated one hundred years of independence—provided a logical patriotic impetus to the genre of historical films. *El Grito de Dolores* (1908) was a reenactment of the events surrounding Father Miguel Hidalgo's call for independence. When *Prisión de Cuauhtémoc* (1918) later appeared on the screens, it revealed a topic to which intellectuals would pay increasing attention not only in the cinema but in music, literature, art, and dance: Mexico's rich Indian past. Still imbued with the tenets of Positivism, the early producers of those historical films regarded them as the "scientific historical truth." Certainly those epics of moving images—a living history—brought the past to a larger Mexican public than conventional historians could ever hope to do in a nation with a large illiterate population. The government quickly appreciated the ability of films to speak to mass audiences. The Ministry of War, as one example, expressed a lively interest in filmic interpretations of the Revolution which kept Mexico in chaos throughout much of the 1910–20 decade, and financed such films as *Juan Soldado, El precio de la gloria,* and *Honor militar.*

The filming of notable current events and historical epics absorbed the Mexican filmmakers for nearly two decades, until they began to appreciate the public's fascination with the "magic" the camera could also perform. They paid greater attention thereafter to fiction and fantasy and consequently moved progressively farther from reality. Doubtless both public and filmmaker reacted against the once sacrosanct Positivist concern for "truth" as one further repudiation of the Porfirian past. By the 1920s, the "hits" produced and exported by Hollywood exerted a growing influence and offered ever sharper competition. The Mexican filmmakers fell under the cultural sway of their northern neighbor and, to the degree that they did, their filmic concern with national reality diminished.

These generalizations about the early Mexican cinema are by no means unique to that country. Broadly speaking they fit the fledgling movie industries wherever they appeared in Latin America. As Hollywood seduced them, the themes, standards, and techniques of the United States became the norms for the Latin Americans. The bulk of the Latin American films were flawed imitations, often unintentional parodies. Fortunately some occasional and notable exceptions to that general trend appeared in the Argentine, Brazilian, and Mexican cinemas. *El compadre Mendoza* (Mexico, 1933) by Fernando de Fuentes, *Ganga Bruta* (Brazil, 1933) by Humberto Mauro, and *Prisioneros de la tierra* (Argentina, 1939) by Mario Soffici stand as three examples of brilliant national films directed by men of extraordinary talent. Their plots treated national themes and unfolded naturally in local environments.

Such delightful exceptions dotted an otherwise bleak cinematic landscape. Indigenous cinemas did not reappear in Latin America until the end of the 1950s, when they emerged almost simultaneously in Brazil and Cuba. Much of Brazil's exciting *Cinema Novo* movement took form outside the traditional film industry. Dedicated young men sensitive to the realities of Brazilian life shaped the new cinema, the most salient characteristic of which was the attention given the brutal poverty of the masses in the midst of potential plenty. The cameras of the young directors concentrated on the two areas of extreme poverty, the *favelas* or shanties of the large cities and the *sertão* or arid backlands of the Northeast. Acknowledged as the first film of this new cinema was *Rio, Quarenta Graus*, directed by Nelson Pereira dos Santos in 1955. The film contrasted the misery of the *favelas* with the affluence of the local elite. In the next decade some talented directors won international reputations for their sensitive and splendid work. None was more original and appealing than Glauber Rocha, whose principal film, *Deus e o Diablo na Terra do Sol* (1963), provided penetrating insights into both the mysticism and reality of the Northeast. An articulate spokesman for the young Brazilian directors, Glauber Rocha defined the Cinema Novo movement in these terms:

> Wherever one finds a director willing to film reality and ready to oppose the hypocrisy and repression of intellectual censorship, there one will find the living spirit of the *New Cinema*.

> Wherever there is a director ready to stand up against commercialism, exploitation, pornography and technicality, there is to be found the living spirit of the *New Cinema*.

> Wherever there exists a director of whatever origin or age willing to place his art and work at the service of the mighty causes of his day, there one finds the living spirit of the *New Cinema*.

> There stands its correct definition and through this definition the *New Cinema* sets itself apart from commercial cinematography which, as an industry, is committed to untruth and exploitation.[1]

The politically conscious Cinema Novo challenged the status quo in Brazil. It advocated a change of the iniquitous institutions which dominated that South American nation.

Unsympathetic to the purposes of the Cinema Novo, the military dictators who seized power in Brazil after April 1, 1964, strangled it with rigid censorship. They frowned upon the frank exposures of the Brazilian reality and regarded filmic discussions of poverty as anathema to the image they wanted to emphasize and threatening to the order they imposed on the nation. Rather than using film to expose the truth, they preferred to encourage a cinema which would hide it, hence a return to the films of escapism, a new emphasis on a dream world. Accordingly, by the end of the 1960s the Cinema Novo movement had passed into history and the Brazilian film industry churned out innocuous soap operas and lulling musicals. Needless to add, the Brazilian films thereafter lacked the originality and significance of those produced during the heyday of the Cinema Novo.

The Instituto Cubano del Arte e Industria Cinematográficos, established March 24, 1959, had created by the mid-1960s the other major innovative filmic trend in Latin America. In the sixteen years since its foundation, the Institute has made more than sixty feature films and five hundred documentaries, a disproportionate number of which have received international awards. One of the major goals of the Institute has been to interpret the revolution; another has been to reinterpret Cuba's past. Profoundly imbued with a sense of history and nationalism, the young Cuban directors constantly express their concern with national roots. For them, film is a significant historical document. Typical of that characteristic is the judgment of Tomás Gutiérrez Alea about his own film, *Una pelea contra los demonios:* "It is an effort to examine our most obscure past, of seeing in a new light our beginnings, still so little examined by history, of becoming conscious of our roots."[2]

The exciting and spectacular *Lucía* (1968), directed by Humberto Solás, combined both the interpretation of the revolution with the reinterpretation of the past, while offering feminine perspectives. Three episodes compose this film, each detailing the participation of a woman named Lucía in Cuba's major struggles: the war for independence in 1895, the fight to overthrow the Machado regime in 1933, and the literacy campaign of the 1960s. A critical and popular success throughout the world, *Lucía* is a model of what the cinema can accomplish in Latin America when it draws upon its own national environment and experience. It simultaneously instructs and entertains, providing a delightful visual and intellectual experience. As the headlines in the movie section of the *Los Angeles Times* proclaimed, "In Castro's Cuba, They Don't Make Films for Fools."[3]

The achievements of the Brazilian and Cuban film movements inspired young directors throughout Latin America who rebelled against the vapid, antinational films their industries insisted on producing. They, too, desired to make films reflecting their national environment, past, and problems, but they confronted at every turn innumerable obstacles: lack of financing, poor and limited equipment, impoverished technical facilities, lack of distribution, an unfriendly press, indifference or fear from the established film industries, and more often than not a hostile government. Despite such monumental obstacles, some original and dedicated filmmakers emerged by the mid-1960s. In the brief span in which they worked, they left some film classics which will serve always as landmarks in the history of the Latin American cinema.

A brief introduction to three significant films and their directors will indicate the concerns and importance of some of Latin America's most introspective recent filmmakers. The Argentines Fernando Solanas and Octavio Getino premiered the lengthy *La hora de los hornos* in 1968 to explain the causes of poverty in Latin America in general and in Argentina in particular. The original colonization had fastened a dependency on Latin America which deepened over the centuries and was probably never stronger than in the twentieth century. The only way to develop, in the filmmakers' opinion, was to decolonize Latin America. In defining the significance of *La hora de los hornos,* Solanas wrote,

Our efforts were to realize a decolonizing film, a film of disruption as compared to the traditional values of American and European cinema; it would not have been a decolonized film if it didn't decolonize its language. A cinema of class: a cinema that chose its public and expression. . . . co-existence with a generalized public. A cinema outside the system, with a specific intention. A cinema of liberation and for liberation, an historic cinema of political-ideological argument. A cinema of profound analysis. A cinema which is very violent not only because it deals with the themes of reactionary violence, but because it is also designed for its expression. . . . It is an intense cinema like an instrument of battle, of concrete struggle. Cinema like a gun, a guerrilla film, a film of and for the masses.[4]

For Solanas and Getino, the film was a catalyst for social and political action, and it aggressively recruited history as its ally.

Miguel Littin, the scriptwriter and director of the Chilean film *El Chacal de Nahueltoro* (1969), wanted his film to "denounce a decaying official state—a social decay" in order to awaken the middle class to its role in creating tragedies such as the one the film described. The film details the true story of an itinerant worker who, while drunk, killed a widow and her five children so that they would not have to continue to suffer the misery in which they were submerged. Littin subtly and sagely attacked the institutions which perpetuate poverty in Chile and made them the real villain of this drama.

A young Bolivian, Jorge Sanjines, directed the powerful *Blood of the Condor* (or *Yawar Mallku* in the original title) in 1969. In it, he boldly dissected the major problem of Indo-America: the relations between the repressed Indian majority and the dominant "Europeanized" minority. His philosophical approach to film emerges from this statement: "I believe that we are no longer interested in film that merely invokes and represents the people, but rather in the experience of film that is made from inside the people, with the participation and the actuation—the action—of the people who have lived their history."[5]

The type of analytical films which these three represent helped to infuse a new excitement into the Latin American cinema. Large crowds packed movie houses and union halls to see and debate *La hora de los hornos.* Sanjines and his friends carried *Blood of the Condor,* a 16 mm projector, and an electric generator into remote Bolivian villages to discuss the film's content with the Indians, many of whom were viewing a film for the first time. The intellectuals discussed and debated film as never before in established journals and new film magazines. Film schools began to multiply.

The excitement proved to be short-lived, partially because of the success of the new cinema. The films questioned too sharply the established order. The elitist governments understood the power of the films, an especially potent means of communication in societies where large numbers of the population were illiterates (or functional illiterates). They promptly moved to suppress any realistic treatment of national problems in the cinema. Chile provides an extreme example of what befell a cinema movement dedicated to explaining national reality and advocating its transformation. One of the first actions of the military chiefs who violently overthrew the constitutional government of President Salvador Allende on September 11, 1973, was to destroy the local film industry, Chile Films. Actors, technicians, directors, and producers either fled or were imprisoned—or in some sad cases were murdered. The military junta prohibited the screening of the films made by Chile Films and appealed to Hollywood to dispatch at once suitable fare for the movie houses. The *Los Angeles Times* jubilantly noted, "Chile Filmgoers Get a Break," while air freight rushed copies of *The Boyfriend, Escape from the Planet of the Apes, Play It Again Sam,* and similar films to Santiago.[6] Chilean screens once again reflected the dream world, fantasies, and cultural tastes of foreigners. Gone—at least temporarily—were the filmic studies of Chilean society and problems, films made by Chileans within a Chilean context about Chile.

Viewed in its broadest perspective, it would seem that Latin American filmmakers seldom have had the liberty to express their artistic and philosophical inclinations. If they do not face the physical repression which Argentine, Brazilian, Bolivian, and Chilean filmmakers have in recent years, they must wrestle with the tough problems of an industry more prone to approve the aping of Hollywood than to encourage the experimentation necessary to nurture originality and a local film idiom. The film industry has been coopted by a bourgeoisie with predictable cosmopolitan tastes and an international lifestyle emphatically sympathetic to patterns and ideas radiating from New York, Paris, or London. Within this broadly sketched background of film movements in contemporary Latin America, the interviews included in this book can be better understood.

The interviews which follow are unique in English. Beatriz Reyes Nevares introduces the American public to thirteen distinguished Mexican directors. She selected them both for their sensitivity and successes. They provide the raw material for an assessment of the avant-garde of the Mexican cinema by expressing their ideas and hopes in these informal conversations. The information provides a much-needed dimension to film studies in the English-speaking world which seldom has paid attention to Mexican films or for that matter to the broader category of Latin American films.

Although the Mexican film industry is one of the oldest and most prolific in Latin America, it has never realized its potential.[7] There have been great Mexican films, of course. *El compadre Mendoza* (1933), *María Candelaria* (1943), *Los olvidados* (1950), *Raíces* (1954), and *Mecánica nacional* (1971) testify marvelously to the possibilities. Still, alongside the acknowledged achievements of Mexican art—the masterpieces of Diego Rivera, José Clemente Orozco, and David Alfaro Siquieros come immediately to mind—or literature—Carlos Fuentes, Octavio Paz, and Agustín Yáñez would be but three of the giants—or even dance—the Ballet Folklórico de México —the cinema remains a promise, a tantalizing expression for the future. Unlike art, literature, and dance, it has not yet found its national roots.

The reasons the Mexican filmmakers have not fulfilled their great potential is perhaps the major theme interwoven in the thirteen interviews which compose this book. Obviously the frustration caused by the difference between what has been accomplished and what could be accomplished agitates these directors. All speak to that subject, commenting on the limited budgets, modest technical equipment, hurried shooting schedules, commercial orientation, influence of Hollywood, and lack of encouragement for creativity. Such a litany could be recited everywhere in Latin America in 1976 with the exception of Cuba.

These directors are in part victims of a cinematic industry whose primary concerns are unabashedly commercial. In their idealism, they often speak of the content of many of the films which they direct as vapid, far removed from the exciting realities of Mexico. They voice a lively concern for a truly national cinema, just as have their counterparts in Argentina, Brazil, Chile, Bolivia, and Cuba. Consciously they yearn for a Mexican cinema. Here the reader will detect a sadness in the apparent contradiction between what the Mexican cinema is and what it might be if these directors could realize their ideals. Their conclusion is that all is not going well within the industry, but they all harbor hopes for change. If and when change does come, it is these directors—or others of their inclinations, talents, and commitment—who will reshape the Mexican cinema. Thus, the interviews which follow provide not only an assessment of the current state of the Seventh Art in contemporary Mexico, they also suggest the contours of its future.

E. Bradford Burns
University of California, Los Angeles

Notes

1. "Cinema Novo vs. Cultural Colonialism. An Interview with Glauber Rocha," *Cinéaste* 4, No. 1 (Summer, 1970): 2.

2. Tomás Gutiérrez Alea, "Presentación de una pelea cubana contra los demonios," *Cine Cubano*, Nos. 78/79/80: 49.

3. Calendar Section, July 13, 1975, p. 36.

4. "Cinema as a Gun. An Interview with Fernando Solanas," *Cinéaste* 3, No. 2 (Fall, 1969): 21.

5. "The Courage of the People, An Interview with Jorge Sanjines," *Cinéaste* 5, No. 2 (Spring, 1972): 20.

6. November 24, 1973.

7. Two splendid analyses of the Mexican cinema are Alejandro Galindo, *Una radiografía histórica del cine mexicano* (Mexico City: Fondo de Cultura Popular, 1968), and Jorge Ayala Blanco, *La aventura del cine mexicano* (Mexico City: Ediciones Era, 1968). Both recognize that whatever the numerous achievements of Mexican filmmakers, they have fallen short of Mexico's potential.

Author's Introduction

The cinema is a contemporary art as well as a very influential one. David Alfaro Siqueiros wished to restore painting to its great medieval role of educating the masses. The cinema now fulfills that mission. Francisco Ayala observes that from the screen we obtain many of our attitudes, our gestures, and various means of confronting others and coexisting with them. "Our world is full of cinematic suggestions," he says; "our language, of allusions. If present-day folklore were investigated, within it would be found, omnipresent, traces of this youthful art."

The cinema, one may say without exaggeration, gathers up the data of reality, elaborates them, and returns them to the public. But the latter, in turn, gathers up these data and absorbs them. From there reality itself receives, as if by a rebound, its own retouched image and, by accepting the alteration, modifies itself. From this point of view the cinema is not only a witness but an agent. It not only reflects the circumstances of an era but in certain ways it contributes to their creation. When the reality presented on the screen does not faithfully coincide with that experienced daily by people, a strange and disturbing phenomenon tends to spring forth: men confuse reality with fiction and think that they are really like the conventionalized characters of the screen. Cinematic conventionalism descends from screen to audience, settles in it, and later accompanies it to the street.

Thus we have a multiple set of mirrors which not only jumble illusions together but which intervene in concrete, tangible acts and in social conduct. The cinema invents its fables with materials it extracts from the real universe, which ends up by believing in the fiction and, having done so, makes it a part of itself. A study of the cinema's influence over rural life in Mexico after *Allá en el Rancho Grande* would be most interesting, although this is offered simply as an example. It is my feeling that that type of life has allowed itself to be affected by the cinema and that it has accepted the screen, in many respects, as a social determinant. Now commonplace, and usually harmful, is the imitating by urban youth of those fictitious young people that they see riding around on motorcycles through the fathomless nights full of sirens, neon signs, violence, and sex. I am not referring precisely to an urge to imitate, which after all is common to all who come into contact with a work of the imagination. Literature is also imitated; the Wertherism of the early nineteenth century constitutes even today an appropriate example of that thesis.

What I am saying is that between the cinema and life there occurs an exchange of reality and fiction. Actors are perhaps the clearest embodiment of this. In our country, actors who portray womanizing and pushy charros on the screen end up carrying pistols at all times, acquiring stables of fine horses, and adopting the attitudes expressed in their film roles—even among their friends and families.

The cinema, then, has enormous powers. They are the same as those of the other arts but far more efficient. Film is a persuasive art par excellence, to a degree unmatched even by television, whose paraphernalia—especially commercials—tend to destroy whatever trace of verisimilitude there is in its images. The cinema is an unfolding of our world, but an obedient and passive unfolding. It properly takes its liberties and launches its images on the tides that lap the shores of the commonplace; it alters these images and again receives them so as to continue, until infinity, its function of reflecting and influencing.

This characteristic of the cinema is the source of its greatest virtue—and of a very great potential danger. If the cinema elaborates our reality it is important that we know how this elaboration is operating. It would be ideal if reality were always elaborated for the better, but this is probably not so.

This book consists of thirteen interviews with as many directors of the Mexican cinema. Now more than ever they are the creators of our cinema. I say that they are now more important as creators than at other times because, as the reader will see, almost all of them are aware of a contemporary phenomenon which confers that responsibility on them: the film director, who used to be constricted by the demands of the producer, the screenwriter, and others, now finds himself alone with his megaphone. Whether this is for better or worse is not a question that will be answered here. The situation is obvious: the director has been liberated. He is truly the author of a work, and in spite of its complexity and the many people who contribute to it, he has claimed for himself—or has received without claiming them—the laurels as well as the brickbats.

Of these thirteen directors of the Mexican cinema, some belong to the "old wave" and some to the "new." It will become obvious in the interviews that they unanimously reject the existence of a coherent, organized movement at the present time. "New cinema" does not strike them as an appropriate expression, although almost all of them agree that today's cinema is unlike that of twenty or thirty years ago. But —as Galindo, for example, says—this is only natural. Times change and artistic standards, or whatever they may be, change along with them.

Thus there are two very distinct generations in the guild of Mexican directors. In his interview, Ripstein clearly identifies them: there are the founders and the successors, and no more. Our cinema is young and its history brief. Now then, what are the differences—and the discrepancies—between one and the other? This is one of the book's main themes, if one can talk in such terms. It seems that, in spite of this division of our directors into only two groups, the story of Mexican film has three chapters. One can speak of the chapter on ingenuous and somewhat rudimentary authenticity; the chapter on the no-longer-so-ingenuous commercialization, technically skilled but artistically impoverished; and the one on the return to primitive sources, with broader horizons and a sharper critical spirit. This outline comprises most of the testimony I have collected and could be restated in commercial terms: in the initial phase, one might say, our film industry struggled to gain internal and external markets; in the next, during the Second World War, it reigned practically without competition in Latin America and the southwestern United States; and now, in the third phase, it is struggling to regain the territory lost due to overconfidence when the war ended, the great filmmaking countries began to produce again, and we fell to the rear.

Very few statements made during the course of the thirteen

interviews can be considered definitive; almost all are moot or could be refuted. One of the solidest is this one: the Mexican cinema has lost its commercial appeal. This is the heart of the matter. The national publics of South America, Spain, and the United States turn their backs on our films, which would suggest the need for a new strategy. But what should we do? Almost all the directors agree that we should improve the quality of our product. But what is to be understood by "improvement?" Some insist that this refers to thematic realism; to others, it means the technical aspect—and so on. It is not easy to obtain a consensus on this subject.

The objective problems of our cinema, according to the directors interviewed in the book, are:

1. The decline of public interest in Mexican films
2. The low quality of these films, which could be one of the causes of that decline
3. The almost total lack of opportunity for new directors, due to union obstacles
4. Low output of films, which results in fewer jobs for the established directors and forces them to shut the doors on the new ones
5. Lack of up-to-date technical capabilities

Among these topics, number 2 is the one that elicits the most comments and directly or indirectly related considerations. The new directors attribute the low quality of our cinema (and some of the older ones agree) to these factors:

1. An excess of commercialism and a corresponding absence of artistic commitment
2. Lack of authenticity and a harmful attachment to a conventionalism that attempts to portray a nonexistent world
3. The greed of the producers who try to save money by any means possible
4. Lack of schools where all cineasts, not only directors, can acquire basic skills, instead of the empiricism that has predominated from the earliest days of our cinema

If one imagines a round table around which are gathered the thirteen directors interviewed in this book, these problems would be the main topic of discussion.

But objective problems are not the only ones discussed in these pages. Subjective problems, that is, those that personally affect the individual director, are also dealt with: their ideas concerning art or the film industry; the anguish caused by the desire to express something artistically; their future plans; what being a director means to each one; and the difficulties that get in their way.

From this perspective the interviews are not only of documentary value but also possess significant human interest. Some of the directors may engage in posturing, but even this has some meaning. Also abundant are spontaneous and pithy statements. All of them portray the man and give a clue to his position. A singularly vehement bitterness—rarely against individuals, but against fads or attitudes—is abundant.

The directors of the old generation have a calm and sensible air about them. They defend their beliefs and interests—which is quite legitimate—with impressively logical arguments. For me they had the charm of evoking—as in the case of Galindo, Fernández, and even Buñuel—times long gone, performers and stories now very distant, in some time warp, on some afternoon at the Parisiana.

The new ones, however, have other weapons, another tone, a new kind of vigor. They are, like all this generation, inclined toward romanticism. They speak with absolute confidence that their statements are valid simply because they utter them. They are the ones who insist most vehemently on authenticity, the tabula rasa that will demolish fetishes and taboos; this, too, is romantic. They believe in the privileges of art, in absolute purity or in close alliance with social questions, and they claim an untrammeled freedom because all human expression should be professed openly. From this it follows that censorship—and almost all of them admit that in Mexico it is quite mild—should seem to them an evil of incalculable magnitude.

The method I followed in deciding which directors to interview was somewhat disorganized. There are figures in the history of our cinema that no one could forget or set aside, such as El Indio Fernández, Alejandro Galindo, and Ismael Rodríguez. Luis Buñuel, with his international fame and his creative and renovative abilities, is likewise a name that no one could easily forget. The choice of these four individuals is sound and no one, I expect, will contradict it. But after them we are no longer on such firm ground—not, of course, because we wish to take anything away from those interviewed here but simply because others are missing who might well have been included. I have completed an interview with Juan Orol, and another with Gavaldón. Alfonso Arau, with his joy in work, his lack of conformity, his satire, and his love of all that is ours, will also speak out in a future book. The same is true of Gonzalo Martínez, whom I interviewed after the final choice had already been made for this book. Gonzalo Martínez, typically northern, is enamored of our country's history and desirous of bringing heroes down from their pedestals and presenting them to the public as flesh and blood beings. The "Super-8 group," which has created so much excitement among the younger generation, should also be a part of that future book. In sum, the omissions are egregious, and I plan to make amends.

But if omissions there are, I do not think I will be chastised for making my choices unthinkingly. The thirteen directors interviewed have a history of impressive accomplishment. Those of a venerable generation do not find it necessary to justify themselves. And, one could almost say, neither do the new ones. It is enough to cite some titles: *En este pueblo no hay ladrones, La mansión de la locura, El castillo de la pureza, Mecánica nacional, El jardín de tía Isabel, Muñeca reina, El profeta Mimí, Los cachorros,* and *Las puertas del paraíso.* These are films worthy of being taken seriously. Some are masterpieces, others not, but all are interesting and decorous. Or some not decorous, a word that alludes to the virtues of discretion and moderation; they are full, it is true, of power, restlessness, the desire to sweep away discredited customs, inept standards, unfounded prejudices.

This second volume I promise myself might record a definite change of direction in our cinema. The Cinematographic Bank has taken steps to correct many past errors. Our cinema seems to be entering a new era in which production—so lean at this time—will not rely on the individual initiative of a handful of gentlemen but on institutional support. For the time being there are new firms, such as Directores Asociados, S.A., which plans to carry out an ambitious filming program and has made stock available to investors. The very same cinematic workers and technicians, who also suffer, obviously, from the low production, are preparing to film "packages" in which each will contribute a part of his normal fees.

The Cinematographic Bank, especially, has found a new dynamism. It finances, promotes distribution, and effectively advertises our films. I have been told—with good reason—that this is all the doing of *licenciado* Rodolfo Echeverría and that it depends on him. In other words, the Bank does not yet depend on an institutionalized apparatus but on the goodwill of one man. It will be necessary, therefore, to create that apparatus or give new life to the one that already exists if that is more convenient. The important thing is that our cinema have before it a long road and, where possible, a secure one.

Licenciado Rodolfo Echeverría, who knows the field as few others do and is also a man of initiative and good intentions, became interested in my interviews even though some of the ideas expressed therein did not exactly coincide with his. From that interest originated the Foreword which he agreed to write, for which I express my profound gratitude.

I also wish to acknowledge the beneficent influence of licenciado Tomás Freymann. It is not a simple matter for a journalist like me, who has to attend to routine work and often domestic matters as well, to hunt down such elusive persons as film directors. One needs patience and perseverance, and Lic. Freymann always encouraged these in me with his consistently optimistic spirit; in addition, through his good offices, he facilitated several of the dialogues that form this book.

Lic. Maximiliano Vega Tato, director of PROCINEMEX, helped me with the filmography of the directors and with the illustrations.

My hopes for this book are modest enough: that it should contribute to a better understanding of the problems of our cinema, and that the readers should learn more about a few of its more important creators. With respect to the first—understanding—I hope that these notes may accomplish something. Perhaps they will give the impression of a more or less confusing discussion, but if one reads attentively, it will be clear that there are ideas that stand out and float over the choppy waters. It is always good to discuss. It is not good to revile and attack, and this hardly ever happens at any point in the interviews. Conflicting ideas are expressed but this was part of the original purpose.

The Mexican cinema has attracted the attention of more than a few critics, some of them highly talented: Emilio García Riera, José de la Colina, María Luisa Mendoza, and Jorge Ayala Blanco are a few of the more important ones who, apart from their work in newspapers and magazines, have published books. I do not pretend to match them. My testimony is marginal. It arises from a zone contiguous to that of cinema—that of the movie fan. Because my opinions—when I risk expressing them—are entirely profane, and thus objective, they may have some value. In addition my questions oscillate between ignorance and candor, and when they hit the mark they can perhaps be credited with efficacy. I should emphasize, however, that my words are the exception; I wanted to let the directors speak and to transcribe their words with the greatest accuracy.

I need only add that, with all their difficulties, these interviews were very pleasant for me. The directors of both generations are very pleasant, courteous, and intelligent people. Their lives are totally involved with the cinema and they talk about it with a passion that may differ in degree among them but is never lacking. They possess knowledge that to me, uninformed as I am, seems esoteric and which they consented to reveal to me in part. Perhaps something similar will occur to the reader; he will feel himself admitted into a milieu which attracts him but of which he is ignorant. This is perhaps another of my book's small virtues.

Emilio Fernández

"Is Mr. Fernández in?"

I don't know how many times I repeated this question. On the telephone, in person, in any number of ways. "El Indio" was never in. He was starting to become a mythical figure. Does El Indio Fernández really exist? Who knows. "He has just gone out." "At around two you'll find him in the restaurant." "We don't know, we don't know, we don't know."

But it became worse once I did find him.

"Mr. Fernández, I would like an interview."

"What for?"

"Well, you see, I am seeing all the important directors of our cinema to have them talk about themselves, the industry . . ."

"A lot has been written about me. Everybody knows what I think."

"But an exclusive interview . . ."

And so it went. I was exhausted. Running after El Indio Fernández at the Churubusco studios, telephone calls to his home, begging people who had some influence on him and might help me out. In short, I tried everything.

Until at last, one day around noon, in the studios . . .

The creator of *María Candelaria* is surrounded by friends, seated at a very long table. It is like a fortress. The group seems impregnable. How can I get him to interrupt the conversation with his friends and say something to me?

But El Indio Fernández isn't as fierce as he is made out to be, or as he wants people to think he is. He sees me from a distance, gets up, and walks toward me. At a small table, next to the one he shares with that chorus, we can talk.

At last . . . And now it happens—as it always seems to in these instances—that I don't know what to ask him. What question would be worthy of this personage of the Mexican cinema? My God, I shouldn't waste this chance. And there he is, with his overwhelming presence, like a Diego Rivera figure that has stepped out of a mural. Massive and immovable. At any moment he might explode, or leave, or do something totally unexpected.

But I have done my homework. For example, his extensive filmography, which comprises thirty-three titles and begins thirty-two years ago with *La isla de la pasión.* A long list of movies among which are such famous titles as *Flor silvestre* and *Enamorada,* as well as *María Candelaria,* which is, deservedly, the classic and most memorable of all Mexican films. On the other hand there are other films on this list that few people remember, apart from scholars like García Riera. Who can remember, for example, *Un día de vida,* which dates from 1950 and in which appeared Columba Domínguez, Roberto Cañedo, and Fernando Fernández? But other films come to mind which are still famous, like *Salón México* and *La red.* Thirty-three films . . . it is easy to say but it represents a lifetime of intense work; of work and friendship, of tireless seeking.

What is El Indio Fernández seeking? Whence comes this grim and silent figure who at this moment sits before me sipping a brandy and with whom I am unable to start a dialogue after many days of trying to obtain it?

It occurs to me to ask him about *La Choca,* his latest film, with which he is still occupied. But I don't know the details. The only thing I know is that Mercedes Carreño acts in it. I fall back on banal, routine questions.

"How did you get your start in films?"

A scene from *La Choca,* a recent Fernández film

Fortunately, El Indio is patient.

"Well, you see . . . In 1928 I was in Hollywood. I was digging ditches near one of the studios. I happened to learn about the editing of an Eisenstein film, *Viva México* . . ."

"But what were you doing in the United States?"

"All right. We'll backtrack a bit. I was born in 1904, on March 26, in a mining town called Del Hondo, in the municipality of Sabinas, Coahuila State. My father was Emilio Fernández and my mother Sara Romo. He was from El Progreso, Coahuila, and she from El Nacimiento.

"All right, but what were you doing in the United States?"

"I had been a supporter of *don* Adolfo de La Huerta, and when he was defeated we had to leave the country."

"So you were a political exile."

"That's right. And I had to earn a living in Los Angeles any way I could. I worked at the most menial tasks . . . As I was telling you, I had a glimpse of Hollywood and it interested me.

It finally interested me because of *don* Adolfo himself, who
told me something I have never forgotten."

"What did de La Huerta tell you?"

"This, more or less," Emilio Fernández frowns to remember.
Then the words come out very slowly. " 'Mexico does not want
nor does it need more revolutions. Emilio, you are in the
mecca of films, and the cinema is the most effective instrument
that man has invented to express himself. Learn to make movies and come back to our country with that knowledge. Make
our very own films and in that way you'll be able to express
your ideas in such a way that they'll reach thousands of people.
You will never have a better weapon than film. No other kind
of message will be more widely diffused.'

"I understood that it was possible to create a Mexican
cinema," continues El Indio, "with our own actors and our own
stories, without having to photograph *gringos* or *gringas* or
tell stories that had nothing to do with our people."

"That reminds me," I say, "of the ambitions of our writers
who, in the mid-nineteenth century, had the same idea. For
instance, I remember *maestro* Altamirano,* who wished to
promote a national literature and invited his colleagues to
utilize our history and our legends for the purpose."

Emilio Fernández nods agreement but otherwise ignores
my observation.

"From then on the cinema became a passion with me," he
continued, "and I began to dream of Mexican films. For six
years I walked around with a script under my arm. I had the
ambition that it would finally be filmed sometime, and I tried
everything. I slept in a small car because I didn't have enough
money for rent. I was very poor but nevertheless I was intent
on creating a national cinema with my script, which was, I
believe, something like the first brick of that edifice.

"The year passed and I returned to the country and went
ahead with my idea. Finally I was going to carry it out, thanks
to my stubbornness and to a law student whom I befriended."

At this point in the discussion Emilio Fernández is more at
ease and more disposed toward a prolonged conversation. His
memory is supplying him with material, and this material is

*Ignacio Manuel Altamirano (1834–93) [*Trans. note*]

undoubtedly quite pleasant. The years of apprenticeship and struggle parade before him, and he lovingly gathers them up with his words.

"That student," he continues, "was quite good looking and very anxious to be an actor. I told him about my ambitions and showed him my script. 'I'll get financing if you're the director and I play the lead,' he finally promised me, and we began to make plans. We went to see General Juan F. Azcárate ..."

"But who was that friend of yours?"

"His name was David Silva. I owe him nothing less than my career. A man of great courage and enthusiasm ... but I was telling you that we went to see General Azcárate. It is true that Raúl de Anda advised me not to come on with a song and dance but to limit myself to telling him that the movie would cost eighty thousand pesos and that he would make a million. The language of figures would have to be the most convincing. We all came out ahead because the general signed up; he made a million, David became an actor, and I became a film director. The upshot was that the three of us got what we each wanted."

"What movie was that?"

"It was my first film, and its name was *La isla de la pasión.*"

La isla de la pasión, which heads Fernández's filmography, was made in 1941, as I have just recalled, and the cast included, besides David Silva, Isabela Corona, Pituka de Foronda, Pedro Armendáriz, Miguel Angel Ferriz, Margarita Cortés, Miguel Inclán, Julio Villarreal, the comedian Carlos López, Chaflán, who was indispensable in that era, the singer Chela Campos, and a few other actors among whom was the director himself, Emilio Fernández. *La isla de la pasión* was well received by the critics, as much for its cinematic merits as for its patriotic ones. I never saw it but I have read that it is based on the terrible experience of a Mexican army detachment that was abandoned on Klipperton Island in 1914; for three years it suffered great privations and endured the ambition and cruelty of a certain Victoriano, who tried to establish himself as a petty tyrant over the unfortunate group.

"Then I made my second film, for Raúl de Anda, entitled *Soy puro mexicano.* Raúl's career—and his fortune—dates from that time ... but we have to proceed a little faster if I'm going to tell you, more or less, my whole story. As you know, I was

Fernández shooting *Zona roja* on location

the first Mexican director with whom Dolores del Río worked. My relative successes and a series of fortunate circumstances offered me that opportunity. *Flor silvestre* was Dolores's first film, and it was made in 1943, based on a screenplay by Fernando Robles that Mauricio Magdaleno and I adapted."

"You and Mauricio Magdaleno have collaborated a number of times, is that correct?"

"Yes. He's a very good writer, and very much ours. I can mention the adaptation of *Río escondido*, the original idea for

Maclovia, the adaptation of *Duelo en las montañas*, the story of *Un día de vida*, of *Islas Marías*, of *La bien amada*, and, finally, many others for which I have counted on him, always with magnificent results. Not for nothing is he considered one of our outstanding contemporary novelists, don't you think? But we were talking about *Flor silvestre*. The cast, of course, was headed by Dolores del Río, along with Pedro Armendáriz, Miguel Angel Ferriz, Mimi Derba, Agustín Isunza, and Armando Soto Lamarina. This film was really an adventure because, as a result of one of those things that occasionally happens, Dolores was not liked here. The day of the premiere, at the Palacio Chino, there were perhaps fifteen people in the audience. We were really very few, and all Dolores's friends. But there were important people. I remember Diego Rivera, José Clemente Orozco, David Alfaro Siqueiros, Manuel Rodríguez Lozano, and Miguel and Rosa Covarrubias. The rest were acquaintances, with a reporter here and there. Also present in the theatre that evening, of May 9, was a radio announcer known as "El Che," whose name was Arturo de Córdoba. Dolores, faced with that emptiness, literally wanted to die, perhaps even kill herself. But between Diego, David, and the others, we cheered her up and convinced her that the whole thing was just a coincidence. Guerrero Galván, whom I had forgotten but who also attended the premiere, loudly declared that with that film was born the Mexican cinema of the Revolution and that Mexico regained its most beautiful woman, who was in addition an excellent actress. The next day an intense campaign was initiated by Arturo on the radio and the reporters through their newspapers, and before the week was out there was standing room only at the theater."

"Tell me about *María Candelaria.*"

"Well, *María Candelaria* was like a logical result of *Flor silvestre.* It was a completely Mexican film, conceived and made for Dolores del Río who had all at once taken her place as our country's distinctive woman. At that time I would have proclaimed her 'the fairest flower of the *ejido.*' I wrote the story of *María Candelaria* on thirteen restaurant napkins and sent it to Dolores on her saint's day because I had no money to buy her flowers. It was in that same year of 1943 and the cast again included Pedro Armendáriz, Alberto Galán, Margarita Cortés, Miguel Inclán, Beatriz Ramos, Rafael Icardo, Arturo Soto Rangel, Julio Ahuet, and Guadalupe del Castillo . . . and, I must remember, *don* Mauricio Magdaleno, whom we just referred to, collaborated with me in the drafting of the outline and its adaptation. We filmed *María Candelaria* in Xochimilco, with many problems caused by the weather and many personal differences. A few good people couldn't go along with the film. It sounded strange to them. It seemed to them—imagine!—exotic and also depressing. They were scandalized and ousted me from the production company, which was Films Mundiales, because I had made 'such shit about Indians.' I had to resolve to starve to death.

"*Don* Agustín J. Fink, the company president, Mrs. Diana Subervielle—later Fontanal's wife—and Felipe Subervielle were unable to console Dolores and me for that disaster, which was already obvious even though the movie had not yet been screened. But then my guardian angel went to work. There was a strike and the theaters didn't have any films to exhibit. *Don* Emilio Azcárraga, the owner of the Alameda Theater, had declared that under no circumstances would our film be shown, and other theater owners followed his lead. The strike put a different light on things and *don* Agustín J. Fink, acting on my suggestion, took advantage of the opportunity and rented the Palacio Theater, which was on 5 de Mayo on a spot which today is a parking lot, to hold the premiere showing of *María Candelaria*. The film was advertised and we had a full house, including real Indians from Xochimilco. During the showing there were catcalls from people who wanted to spoil the show because they were professionals and were most certainly envious. The Indians quieted them down, and at the end a gentleman with a foreign accent stood up and shouted for the director and the actress. It was Mr. Oumansky, the Soviet ambassador, who died in a plane crash shortly after that. Thanks to Oumansky and his great personality our *María Candelaria* was off and running, and it was sent, I don't know how, to the Cannes Film Festival. From there we brought back every prize and a comment from Georges Sadoul who said he had been able to perceive 'the darkness and the light of Mexico through *María Candelaria*.'"

But for a few minutes El Indio Fernández's friends have been calling him from their table, and El Indio's attention is divided. He feels like returning to the gathering and decides to cut the interview short.

"We can continue some other time," he says as if to console me.

But it was not possible. And after all it was not really necessary because what El Indio knows about the cinema wouldn't fit in one or even two volumes, and because what I wanted him to tell me is sufficient for this brief interview.

2

 Alejandro Galindo

"There is no such thing as a 'new' cinema . . ."

Alejandro Galindo, blunt and aggressive, stares at me firmly through the column of steam rising from his cup of coffee.

"That slogan," he continues, "has been concocted purely for public relations purposes. That's all. Films are made during a specific period, and from the point of view of that period they are always new. But there is nothing exceptional in this."

"Very well, there's more to my question. I was going to bring up other subjects. I wanted to talk about the young directors and the difficulties they have breaking into the industry. I've heard many complaints. They say that the union or association that Rogelio González presides over is like a mafia which doesn't give any of them a chance. I have also listened to complaints from other directors who enjoy the prestige of being long-established in our film industry. They allege there is no work, that opportunities are few. What is the actual situation?"

Galindo remains silent for a few seconds until some street noise dies down. It is quite pleasant in this restaurant on Juárez

21

Avenue, although the noise of car horns can still be heard. It is a place with checkered tablecloths, full of Italians. The creator of *Los Fernández de Peralvillo* is a regular customer here, coming over every afternoon to write.

"If you wish," he says finally. "I can talk about the subject. It is a complicated business and I don't think the public would be interested in it. People don't care about labor conflicts and contractual problems. But they could be of some interest to young, aspiring directors."

"Is it more difficult to break into films now than in the past?"

"Well, I think it's always been the same. In this sense, films are no different from any other art. Establishing a reputation entails the same problems for a young cineast as for a young writer or painter."

But *don* Alejandro is not satisfied with his own answer and begins to quality it.

"Although it is true," he goes on, "that there are specific dangers in the cinema. Look here, if a new author takes his book to an editor, the only issue is the quality of the work and the publication costs, which could be fifteen, twenty, or fifty thousand pesos. We, on the other hand, deal with much higher figures, and the work, that is to say, the film, isn't something tangible which can be judged beforehand. It is only in the planning stage. There is no manuscript, as is the case with books. You can well imagine: the investment is considerable and the outcome is completely unpredictable ... True, the young aspirant is never completely unknown. His capabilities are more or less a matter of record. But it is impossible to know how his film is going to turn out, that film which is going to cost so much."

"What was your first film?"

"Didn't you say that you wanted to talk about up-and-coming directors and their start in the industry?"

"Yes, but I also want to know about Alejandro Galindo. I think the other subject can be dealt with in the course of the conversation."

A gesture of resignation.

"Well, my first full-length motion picture—because I had previously made some documentaries—was called *Almas rebeldes*. I filmed it with Raúl de Anda in 1939."

"Did you start out as a director?"

"No, not exactly. I began like everyone else . . . in the United States working in a film laboratory and studying dramatic art at night. I studied writing, acting, set construction, and other similar things. I certainly can't complain about the facilities. I had everything I wanted. They lent me books and anything else you can think of. I really milked the *gringos* as far as knowledge is concerned."

"And who produced *Almas rebeldes*?"

"The same Raúl de Anda."

Tom Mix and His Three Hundred Cossacks

There is a faraway look in Alejandro Galindo's eyes, toward the past.

"Raúl de Anda was a movie buff. He had a stable with forty-two cows. I remember very well because he pawned those animals to finance the film. He had had a small role in an Arcady Boytler movie called *Mano a mano.*

"Raúl de Anda," continues my interviewee, "had also been in one of Tom Mix's shows. You do know who Tom Mix was, don't you? Well, he was a very brave cowboy—something like the Lone Ranger. And this cowboy had a troupe that toured the United States. It was called 'Tom Mix and His Three Hundred Cossacks.' There were riders from Arizona, Nevada, Wyoming—from everywhere except Russia. Among them were about two hundred charros from here, from Mexico . . ."

"How was our cinema in those days, in the late thirties?"

"Very *simpático*. It functioned on pure Mexican courage."

"Where were the studios?"

"In the vicinity of today's Chapultepec Theater. Around where they later put up the statue of Ariel, which today is in the Churubusco Studios. Those studios, the old ones, belonged to a Mr. Abitia, a good friend of General Obregón, whom he filmed quite a bit. Today those films would constitute a valuable documentary."

"Not too long ago Carmen Toscano was telling me that our cinema began with newsreels with the object of creating a historical record."

"That's true. It's what Salvador Toscano did. And besides their other merits, one has to recognize the great courage and physical stamina of those precursors ... Just imagine what those cameras weighed and how difficult they were to operate."

A Digression on Fame

"Were those the first studios in Mexico?"

"No. There were others, for example those belonging to Germán Camus and Co., located in the Revillagigedo area. That gentleman imported European films. Someone—I don't know who—interested him in financing a film, which was the first *Santa*. This was still during the mute or silent film era, whatever you want to call it. The star was Elenita Sánchez Valenzuela, a student at the Miguel Lerdo de Tejada School. You can't imagine the ruckus that was kicked up when that girl became an actress. No one could conceive of a student exposing herself to that contaminating atmosphere ..."

"Did you know her?"

"Of course I knew her. Yes, indeed. She was gorgeous, but my eyes could not aspire to look into those eyes." Galindo's expression becomes one of mock disenchantment.

"She was obsessed with her celebrity status," he explains. "That was already happening. It isn't precisely the cinema that turns one's head—it is the fame that it brings about. Personally, I think that fame is very deceptive. Man thinks he is fulfilled by fame—he thinks it gives him impunity and wisdom. But this is not true. Fame enables people to know of you, to point you out, to have them whisper your name as you walk down the street. But when dealing with other matters it is of no use at all. Put yourself in the most prosaic situation—business. No one gets a reduction in the price of a piece of land because of fame. And fame does not make us more ingenious or sharper in a discussion of other topics. Fame has nothing to do with ideas. Frequently, however, those who have achieved it become unbalanced."

"And in the cinema it is very easy to attain, isn't that true? What I mean is that, apart from the difficulties in establishing

A scene from *Y la mujer hizo al hombre*

oneself, the film industry offers a great deal of popularity—not only for actors and actresses but also for directors."

"I've seen some directors wind up in the booby hatch—a mental institution, an insane asylum—and this is because the public attributes to its so-called idols certain characteristics they don't possess."

The Cinema, Politics, and Bad Producers

"What does the cinema mean to you?"

By Galindo's expression, I sense that I have brought up one of his favorite subjects.

"For me . . . what can I tell you? Apart from the passion it provokes, it constitutes an obsession you can scarcely imagine. Because the cinema could be a very useful instrument to educate the people, to draw them out of the confusing circumstances that presently afflict them and of which they're not aware. And the truth is that it seems to have rejected that task."

"What is the reason?"

"The attitude of the politicians. The clash of ideas makes it impossible for certain things to be said on the screen, for certain language to be used ... It is caught between capitalism and the left."

"I understand that some subjects are considered dangerous by one group or another, and then they opt for silence. But tell me, *don* Alejandro, is there no country in which the cinema fulfills its social responsibility?"

"Well, I don't dare say. There are cinemas I don't know anything about."

"Could the ideal be a cinema such as Costa Gavras's in Greece?"

"Well, he attempts it and it is a laudable and admirable thing. More than admirable, for me personally it is to be envied. Pontecorvo also ... But look here, there is a circumstance that should be taken into account, in addition to the responsibility to his peers that any person has who uses any medium of mass communication. It is a circumstance of a practical nature, of personal convenience: if a film does not say something, it is lost. It's good to remember that every year some two thousand or twenty-five hundred films are released. It is difficult to leave a trace. It is necessary then to shake up the public."

"What is it that shakes up the Mexican public?"

"Very basic, simple things; and for a very simple reason: our unfortunate people are submerged in a sea of confusion. It is the most disastrous thing that could happen. Perhaps part of the fault may be found in our character; there might be other factors that have not been carefully studied. It is true that we have been traumatized since the Conquest and that throughout history we have been victimized by countless deceptions. This is all true, but in addition there are other things. We suffer from a radical individualism. We completely shut ourselves off from others. Then follows that indifference and distrust of politics, because politics is, above all, a community of ideas.

The Mexican is incapable of sharing anything, and politics therefore matters nothing to him. Because of that, Mexican films have opted for superficiality."

"But doesn't all this result in downgrading the people and preventing them from growing mentally?"

"Just one moment. I'm not saying that socially significant pictures should not be made. What I'm saying is that they're not being made because there is a certain involuntary mis-alliance . . . The fear of the producers, the public's indiffer-ence . . ."

"Then they can and should be made?"

"That they should be made is beyond dispute. At this mo-ment the social aspect is the important thing. The political aspect in film is what the people are demanding."

"Then if Mexico continues in its inertia it could even lose its foreign markets. As it is, we are not doing as well as before in those markets . . ."

Galindo makes an affirmative gesture. A waitress brings him a fresh cup of coffee.

"Well, it would be a matter of attempting it," he finally says. "Of attempting to have our cinema bring together a lot of dispersed ideas, many seemingly forgotten concepts . . . Per-haps it would be good if someone were to attempt a change of attitudes; that in place of feeling a type of self-contempt, we should feel an amorous pain."

"Do you think such a thing is possible? With the producers we endure . . . Some quite worthy of consideration but who nonetheless prostitute themselves . . ."

"It's not that bad . . . They have to earn a living," pronounces Galindo. "Perhaps I too have prostituted myself."

"Speaking of that, what is your worst movie?"

"I don't know. I've made a number."

"I remember some very good ones, like *Una familia de tantas* and *Campeón sin corona.*"

"Those are the type of films we have to cultivate," com-ments Galindo, returning to the subject we had apparently abandoned. "Those films are capable of reaching the people and leaving a message, of gradually forming a conscience. But one film, like one swallow, does not a summer make. It is lost, no matter who makes it. What is important is to instill a new attitude throughout the industry. To create a movement that is trying to achieve something specific . . . And that, as you will understand, cannot be accomplished by one man alone. It is a matter for many people."

"Of a system."

"Of course, of a system. The enterprise suggests strong financial backing and many people . . . Without being mathematically precise, we could think of ten directors, ten writers . . ."

"Are there none?"

"Don't ask me to express such opinions. I refer in the abstract to that necessity."

"But then we would arrive at a cinema . . . how should I put it? . . . at a *directed* cinema, with just one idea and one goal. It would be static and dry. A government-run movie industry. The more fastidious would not participate . . ."

"Because they're idiots. Very well, in the first place it wouldn't necessarily have to be official. It would take off from a basic idea. This is all. And I tell you, if they didn't participate it would be from idiocy, because a lot of money could be made from such a cinema."

"But one thing at a time. You were telling me, *don* Alejandro, that a group of ten directors and ten writers would be necessary. Don't you think that ten actors would also be needed?"

"Actors can be made. That's no problem."

"Then why aren't some manufactured? The truth is that today there is no Pedro Armendáriz or . . ."

"There are as many Pedro Armendárizes as you want."

"Where are they?"

"Listen, I can't make them myself. That's why I was telling you that this is not a project for just one man . . . It's best we don't get off the subject. We were talking about a *directed* cinema. I have to be precise about the use of that word because it could sound bad yet it doesn't imply such terrible things. What I mean by it is that our cinema should set a goal for itself and that this should be that of creating a consciousness in our people. A consciousness of their nationality . . . Look here, we tend to talk a lot about the nation; we do everything 'for Mexico' and 'in the name of Mexico.' But we don't endow those phrases with substance. They are nothing more than verbal formulas which the wind tends to carry off. It all sounds so ethereal . . . It would be good if we specified and pinned down concrete ideas: why is Mexico a nation? In what does Mexico consist? Where does it come from, where does it want to go? Films could serve to answer these questions. Not classroom answers. They would give indirect, intelligent, understandable answers but without the appearance of indoctrination. Films could make the Mexican sincerely love his country, with an active love. Right now we fool ourselves into thinking we love it but rarely do we show it with deeds. We only say it, but our actions do not conform to the phrase."

"Our people love soccer and the Virgin of Guadalupe."

"And that is enough. 'On December 12 I go to the *Villa* and with this I am at peace with my Mexican conscience.' "

"And May 10* is another key date."

"Well, that's another story. But I'm going to tell an anecdote which shows very clearly the way we are, our way of vituperating ourselves, of self-discrimination, it could be said . . . Do you want to hear it? Do we have time?"

"All the time you want, *don* Alejandro."

"Very well then, here goes: I have just completed a movie called *El juicio de Martín Cortés.* What is attempted in it, and I don't know if I succeeded, is to tell the Mexican: 'Forget the Spaniard, forget the Indian; you should understand that you represent a new nationality.' This is the film's message. In it appear Cortés, Malinche, and their son, who is precisely *don* Martín. Well then, it so happens I have a friend in Veracruz who keeps up with my work. And this friend, in turn, knows many students, and one fine day he began to tell them the plot. He explained Martín Cortés's genealogy to them. 'He is the first Mexican in history,' he told them. 'Ah,' they answered, 'then he was the first son of a bitch.' "

"Is our inferiority complex or self-contempt that bad?"

"This is repeated constantly in other ways. For example, imagine this scene. The lady of the house says to the maid: 'So your cousin had a baby . . . Congratulations to her. Was it a boy or a girl? It must be very beautiful.' But again comes the disclaimer that spoils the compliment and which shows the true

*Mother's Day [*Trans. note*]

A scene from *El juicio de Martín Cortés*

nature: 'Yes, but he is dark.' The complex appears again . . .
And on so many other occasions. It could even be dangerous.
Go on imagining. Now we are witnessing another scene. It is
a street. There is a traffic accident. The protagonists argue. If
one of them refers to the other's mother, most certainly nothing will happen. The whole thing will end up in insults. But one
must be careful if, instead of the familiar phrase, this pair of
words should be uttered: 'filthy Indian.' Then who knows what
might happen. The victim becomes infuriated and loses control of himself."

"Well, yes, of course . . ."

"But in sum, this was a small digression. Now do you understand why I speak of a *directed* cinema?"

"And what would that cinema be like?"

"I don't have all the answers. Our ten directors and ten
writers would have to be profoundly critical. They should be
very knowledgeable not only about their profession but also
about sociology and politics."

"To date hasn't the only objective of the Mexican cinema
been to make money?"

"Not always. There have been some well-intentioned attempts, especially in the beginning. Now, during this chat we have recalled a film that is very Mexican, judging from the title, and which actually is: *Mano a mano.* We should also mention *Santa* and works like *La parcela,* the novel by López Portillo y Rojas that was brought to the screen as *La posesión.* In sum, they were attempts, as *El prisionero 13* and *El compadre Mendoza* had been before them, at making films that were Mexican in every way. Of course, as the decade of the thirties progressed, the cinema gradually detached itself from reality, because reality was too heterogeneous, too restless, and in some ways still too turbulent. The cinema extracted the superficial, familiar parts of that reality and with them began a gigantic juggling act. It elevated conventionalism to the level of profound definition. And the public joined in the game and declared itself satisfied with conventionalism."

"It was a game of deception. That Mexico was not Mexico, but the people, who should have known better, swallowed the bait."

"That's how it happened, more or less."

Five Years of Revelry

"Then came the five years of World War II," continues Alejandro Galindo. "For us here in Latin America, that conflagration was none of our business. It was an event that had some interest but no more. An event that brought a lot of money to our shores and a great number of adventurers of every kind. There were people like King Carol of Rumania and a large number of blond vamps. A hundred nightclubs opened and in them the capital began an artificial though attractive life. We created the illusion of cosmopolitanism. All the world's languages were spoken at the bar in the Sans Souci or Ciro's. Enormous fortunes changed hands with the greatest ease. Speculation was the order of the day, as well as loose morals. In a word, corruption had arrived. And corruption . . . Haven't you read my book entitled *Una radiografía del cine mexicano?* . . . Well, in it I talk about all these things. I'll give you a copy. I was telling you about corruption, and the cinema is very vulnerable to it. The cinema became corrupted. It was a goal for profiteers and phonies. Everyone who wanted to make investments promising quick returns got into the business. They would strut around passing themselves off as producers or what have you. The cinema was a convenient point of departure. It was the road to wealth, social brilliance, and psychological satisfaction. And, in effect, our cinema was loaded down with strange individuals who had no wish to convey a message to the public. They cared not a whit for any possible messages. Something else attracted them. And our cinema dedicated itself to singing meaningless songs and to narrating cloying love stories when that of the United States and other countries was documenting the horrors of war. What happened then? Well, the publics of Latin America suffered from great confusion. At first they accepted the superficial Mexican filmmaking because the war, I repeat, did not concern them. But later, after the war ended and great films began arriving from Hollywood, Great Britain, Italy, from Russia and Japan, from France and the new socialist countries, the panorama initiated a change that had to affect us in some way. And it did affect us, don't you doubt it. It affected us and we are still suffering the consequences of that blow. It produced a loss of markets and the public became aware of other forms of filmmaking. Of other ways of capturing truth and projecting it on the screen. The public placed conventionalism in a more appropriate spot."

"And we are still in that situation, true?"

"Yes, we are still at that some point, more or less, although it seems that something is beginning to move."

Beatricita's Tacos and Amateurishness

"Listen *don* Alejandro, am I to understand that amateurishness is one of the most objectionable defects of our cinema? Because you have just said that our producers are amateurs and I imagine that everybody else at one time or another followed suit."

"Concerning producers there is no doubt. Did you know something? Even Beatricita, the illustrious creator of the tacos that carry her name and who is established on Uruguay Avenue ... Well, even she has been a movie producer. She produced *Cielito lindo,* simply because she liked that song very much and she had never appeared in a movie. Then someone talked her into backing a film with that song as the theme. And there you have her—*doña* Beatricita, so well known, so admirable in many ways but so removed from the cinematographic medium, but a producer. A very 'folksy' chiseler had induced her to get involved in such a business."

"And is there amateurishness in other areas of the cinema?"

"In all of them. In the technical aspect as well. Perhaps for that reason our films may have the greatest merits in many respects but technically they are always inferior to Hollywood's, which are faultless. It is simply that we don't get along with technical matters, which require mental rigor and dedication. It is at the opposite pole from our 'it'll work itself out' attitude."

"To sum up, *don* Alejandro, the war brought us a false euphoria that took us to the edge of corruption from which we still haven't freed ourselves."

"More or less that is so. That corruption was the cause of an endless series of empty films that the public accepted because it is entirely depoliticized. Thus it frivolously accepts the prize fighter films, like those that come to us from Hong Kong and the ones that feature violence for its own sake, etc."

And Back to the Problem of the Union

"Is it in order to prevent amateurishness that the unions are so rigid and refuse to accept new people?"

"As you can see, we have returned to the initial theme ... Well, yes, if you wish, let's talk about it. In the first place, in the *very* first place, there is this: the union is a resistance organization, and we have been told that this is an industry and that it should be measured with the same yardstick applied to all industries. The cinema is not an open field, like painting. Here we all have an economic responsibility that goes beyond our personal interests. The union has to look out for everybody. For the executive, the electrician, the set designer—for everyone."

"But don't you think that the new people can respond just as well to those demands and shoulder the responsibilities that the industry signifies?"

"Wait a minute, let's go one step at a time. Right now we're talking about the union. The obligation of this kind of organization, or in other words, one of its obligations, is to satisfy the manpower needs of the industry it belongs to. In addition to being a resistance organization, the union is a cog within the production mechanism. And I'm not referring only to movie production but to any kind of product. If the industry requires a certain number of personnel it is the mission of the union to supply them—and to supply qualified people."

"But how is that union harmed if new elements are allowed in?"

"It is harmed, simply and obviously, because there is no work."

"Then there is insufficient production?"

"At the moment, the directors' list contains a hundred and thirty-six names, and some twenty-five films a year are being made."

"In this respect, what was the best period?"

"From what we've discussed you can guess it was during the war."

"What percentage of the directors work regularly?"

"Well, in terms of percentages, I can't tell you."

"But are there directors who haven't worked for a number of years?"

"Many, many."

"Then is it very difficult to receive a directing assignment?"

"You have no idea. At this moment, Beatriz, in my house we are suffering an agonizing problem. I don't know, nor does anybody else, what film I'll be making in the near future. When? With whom? These are urgent questions, but still there are no answers. But it is not something that concerns only the director. It is a question of the cinema, and the cinema is important in contemporary society. The artist has always invested himself with that importance, and in our day the cinematic art has assumed the role that in former days was held by painting, the theater, or literature."

"What do you think of television?"

"Well, television . . . I don't wish to use strong language but there is no choice. It could be very useful but it puts itself at the service, simply and obviously, of the manipulative tactics of public opinion."

"Has television greatly harmed directors?"

"I don't think so. Many of them have found work in that industry."

"It has helped, then, to resolve the unemployment problem . . ."

"Which, I repeat, is an agonizing problem."

"Tell me a bit more about this situation."

"Well, look. There is a circumstance I don't want to overlook. Mexico is the poorest of the filmmaking countries. It is the poorest in terms of personnel. As far as the number of films it offers the fewest opportunities. Between the years '69 and '70 thirty directors debuted among us, thirty. Can you imagine what this means? Thirty in the poorest country, while the debuts in Hollywood, Paris, England, Rome, the Soviet Union, India, Japan, putting them all together, do not come to that figure."

"And how is the work of those new directors evaluated?"

"Go to the movies yourself and see them. What would I know?"

"But they've made very good movies."

"That is a very respectable criterion. But many of them, even if they made good movies, are not working now. There is little work for the old ones, for those in the middle, and for the young ones."

"Why aren't there producers who will make films?"

"There are many circumstances preventing it. We've already seen that the markets have shrunk. On the other hand, the new conditions set down by the Bank do not satisfy many people."

The Director's Personality

"How many films have you directed that were financed by the Bank?"

"In the new epoch, two. By 'new epoch' I mean the adminis-

tration of licenciado Echeverría. But of course the Bank is a
twenty-year-old institution. If you ask me about that entire
period, to tell the truth, I wouldn't know what to answer . . .
But let me emphasize that the director doesn't deal directly
with the Bank. One of those two films I mentioned fell into my
hands because Yolanda Ciani and Carlos Bracho, who had both
been dealing with that institution, asked me to direct it. The
other one is *El juicio de Martín Cortés,* which I already mentioned to you. This work has been made possible thanks to the
enthusiasm of a group from Técnicos y Manuales. Facing the
lack of work, they organized and pooled their efforts. I contributed half. And I'm not referring to financial resources, because if I were able to take care of half the financing, I'd be in
a business other than films."

"I assure you that you'd do no such thing."

"Really, Beatriz, really."

"But I'd like you to talk about yourself. About your beginnings."

"That is not important."

"What do you mean a director's personality is not important? When people go to the movies what they want to see is
Fellini or Antonioni or Bergman or Buñuel or Galindo."

"Fellini was good in his first two films, but now—God help
him! . . . No, look that's not the way things are. I think that a
while ago we dealt somewhat with the topic. The cinema has
been lowering itself and brought us all down with it. It is not
a cinema that belongs to us."

An Artificial and Inauthentic Cinema

"It is not ours," continues Galindo, "for a simple reason: it
doesn't deal with the things that are important to us. It has
confined itself to sensationalism and technique. We are in the
reign of sham and special effects. There are films that no one
understands. They are set in unrealistic settings full of alumi-
num, china closets, lighting without visible source. Actions lack
logical motivations. I repeat, they are not understood but this
in itself is a quality. If no one understands them, good. They
don't state problems related to human beings. They are hybrid

products, and consequently they cannot interest the spectator beyond the *appearance*, in other words what the eye success-fully captures. You were asking me why no new idols are made, why great figures are not created, great actors and actresses. Well, consider this: how are people going to accept an artist if they don't see him as a human being? The good old days of the twenties and thirties have definitely passed into history, the days when the great idols really existed for the spectators, as human subjects."

"So the epoch of stars is gone."

"The stars have another enemy, which is television. In general contemporary life, with its rushing about and its anxieties, takes away the pleasure of contemplation. A pretty girl walks by and we of course admire her but we no longer have the leisure to do it properly."

"And what effect has television had?"

"By getting us too close to the stars. They are no longer intangible or unreachable, as they were in the beginning. That's precisely why they were called stars. They aren't ideal-ized beings that appear like shadows on a screen. They are flesh-and-blood beings, and every day we can watch them in a soap opera. They continue to be very attractive girls, but there are many more like them."

"Wouldn't you like to work in television?"

"Of course I would. Aside from the money, one can also do interesting things. Everything related to stage art interests me. I am not indifferent to any of its manifestations."

"Listen, *don* Alejandro, are there also mafias of cameramen, scriptwriters, and all of those specialties?"

"Don't call them mafias, Beatriz. They aren't really that. We should realize that we live in a capitalist country and that the film industry partakes of that character. Then we are obligated to survive. And we also have the obligation of protecting the industry. These imperatives don't always work against the newcomers. Look at me, for example: in practically every film I have used some novice, and this for the good of the industry. It is necessary to nourish it with materials, talents, with factors that will replace the old and worn out. Giving work to a young-ster is the same as buying a floodlight. It renovates some part of this enormous mire that is filmmaking."

"That may not be a very humane consideration, but at least it is practical."

The Cinema Is a Commercial Matter

"It is getting late *don* Alejandro, and I can't take another cup of coffee."

"But the conversation has been useful. At least that's what I hope."

"Of course it has. And I don't like to interrupt it. But let's sum up. The new directors, then, encounter obstacles because the industry cannot absorb them. There are too many directors and too few films. Why don't the producers work more? The other day I was reading, I think in *Novedades,* that what happens is that they have never bothered to reinvest their earnings in the same business. They have others, and it is to these that they channel the money they have made in films."

"Very well, but the conditions prevalent in today's movie industry make investment riskier every day."

"Due to distribution?"

"Because of distribution and exhibiting. There are many interests."

"How could this state of affairs be corrected?"

"That is little less than utopian—trying to take commercialism out of films."

"When you made *Almas rebeldes* weren't there commercial considerations?"

"Of course. The same as now, but the amounts were smaller. That's all. As I tell you, we are dealing with something utopian. Our industry was small, very miserable, incipient. But everything was proportional. In those times investing in a film was also a very great risk."

"How could the current inertia be remedied? Couldn't there be new producers?"

"They could also change conditions for us."

"What might that change be like?"

"What I can tell you is that, things being what they are, we directors could never obtain a loan from the Bank. We can't give them any assurances. The Bank is a serious institution and

A scene from *Ante el cadáver de un líder*

it would be justified in denying us financing. It lends money when it knows that there is a guarantee."

"But it should also insist on quality, don't you think?"

"First we should agree on what constitutes quality."

"I refer to the 'wrestler' movies, for example."

"What's so bad about them? There are other things no one notices—in magazines and popular novels, for instance. With the advantage that the movies require more effort on the part of the spectator in order to consume the product. Imagine yourself, you have to decide to go to the movies tonight, you have to get ready, convince your husband, take the car, find a parking space. On the other hand, to buy a Corin Tellado publication the only thing you have to do is spend ten seconds at the corner newsstand. You, Beatriz, do not go to see the wrestler movies because you are not going to go to so much trouble over such a little thing. On the other hand, it is possible that at any given moment you will buy one of those little novels."

"All right, but many people do go to see The Saint."

"Certainly, because the people are interested in him and take him to their hearts. But I don't think it's worthwhile to criticize those films. The ones that deserve criticism are those that are passed off as big productions. Not the others. They're simple films, for kids."

"But the poor kids!"

"Don't you also get yourself into a utopian attitude! For seventy-five years the cinema has been dealing with laughter, tears, suspense, with everything. I was telling you that only by liberating it from the commercial angle could we make it a complete cultural agent."

"Very well, but finally, does one win or lose in the cinematic adventure?"

"The producer usually has nothing more than a desk. He could be rich but his private assets are one thing and those of the corporation or whatever, through which he participates in the industry, are quite another. He has nothing except perhaps a secretary and an adding machine, over which, naturally, no one can slap an attachment. The only thing he owns is the negative, which can be distributed. But that is all."

"And then what happens?"

"The distributor's lack of resources induces him to trickery. For instance he asks for a million for a film and he ends up spending seven hundred fifty thousand pesos. The rest, down the hatch."

"But that's very wrong."

"In addition it results in many reductions in the quality of the movies because the director finds himself with one watchword: save money. Instead of forty extras he has to make do with ten. Instead of five weeks' shooting he has to do it in two. And a few movies are made like that. And this is obvious in everything. Look, as a woman you'll understand this: previously the actress's wardrobe was especially created for the film. A designer was paid who came up with the most adequate clothing for the film and the star's personality. If that clothing happened to be attractive, the feminine public was in the palm of our hand. But now the stars are dressed off the rack, and women, when they go to the movies, feel somewhat cheated. The reaction is inevitable: 'You are offering me,' they say to the star, 'the same thing I have in my closet and what my friends wear.' And another of the cinema's attractions is lost. An attraction, you may say, that is quite run-of-the-mill and not too subtle, but which in the past proved effective."

Delicious Kitsch

"Are the movies really that influential?"

"You can't imagine! The ambition of housewives to have a complete, modern kitchen was born in movie theaters."

"Yes. I remember those movies of the forties, which were horrible. Very kitschy, no? Those movies in which the rich family's residence always had a staircase with two banisters and gauze curtains."

"That all goes with the times. We shouldn't pretend that people should go along with our personal tastes. They are not obligated to think as I do. As far as I'm concerned I confess that I have made deliberately kitschy movies."

"Like what?"

"La vida de Agustín Lara, to begin with. *Corona de lá-grimas,* which is a monument. A last and more recent example, *María.* And that's because the novel is kitsch, extreme kitsch. It's very well written but it's kitsch, the same as *Camille."*

"All right, but we were talking about the producers' niggardliness."

"There was a time in which they skimped even on sets, in spite of their importance."

"Why is the set so important?"

"It is a formidable support for the director. It helps to create the atmosphere. The director, as I think I told you, is not a magician or a demigod. For instance, imagine that we wished to make a ghost movie using as a setting a Social Security clinic, one of those very modern ones, so full of sunlight, so shiny. Isn't it true that it would be difficult? You would almost have to be a genius to achieve an atmosphere of terror in such a setting."

"Then they save on the wardrobe, sets, cameramen . . . Do people like Gabriel Figueroa work little?"

"Of course, because they charge too much."

"For you, the directors, does some kind of tariff exist?"

"Yes. The minimum amount we are paid per film is the sum of thirty-three thousand pesos."

It is definitely late. Alejandro Galindo, with his beret and his festive, austere face, could continue talking indefinitely. And I could go on listening but there are space limitations. I say goodbye to him. A very cordial man, very aggressive, very full of ideas and restlessness—one of the great builders of our cinema. I have a number of doubts. It could be that the discussion contained contradictions and vague points. I prefer to leave them thus. That is the way conversations are, and I do not expect that anyone can arrive at absolute truth or perfect agreement. I want each interview to speak freely of the cinema and its problems.

3

 Ismael Rodríguez

"When do you think the Mexican cinema really began? In what does the Mexican cinema consist?"

"I think that Emilio Fernández initiated it and that Alejandro Galindo and I continued it. In our films we have tried to reveal the problems that affect Mexicans, our way of thinking, and the character that distinguishes us."

I am with Ismael Rodríguez in his office at the producers' condominium on División del Norte Avenue, across the street from the Olympic swimming pool. It is an office out of science fiction, full of tape recorders, speakers, and other equipment I cannot identify. The director of *Nosotros los pobres* is a sturdy man, greyish and fast-talking.

What he has just told me about the origin of our cinema and the three personalities that instilled it with its present character is the absolute truth—not just because he says so but because there is other identical testimony which I have gathered in my interviews. El Indio Fernández, Alejandro Galindo, and Ismael Rodríguez are the three founders of the Mexican

45

cinema although none of them made the first film. Along with Fernando de Fuentes, whose pioneering role as director and producer cannot be disputed, they constitute an inescapable tetralogy for anyone who pretends to explain our cinema. Speaking of De Fuentes it is enough to recall *El compadre Mendoza,* based on a story by Mauricio Magdaleno. This movie, filmed in 1933, is not only one of the earliest but also one of the films that began the authentic Mexicanist series.

"Everyone says that you are a complete cineast because you are not only an accomplished director but a master of other technical details."

Ismael Rodríguez nods agreement before I finish my sentence.

"That is true," he answers. "I could also tell you that directing films isn't the most satisfactory work for me, although to the public it is the most visible. In reality the only thing I don't know how to do in moviemaking is to manufacture the raw film, or the celluloid on which the photographs are recorded. Everything else I know, and one of these days I'll take off for Guadalajara to learn that celluloid business. But I have been a projectionist, editor, laboratory technician, sound technician, cameraman, screenwriter, distributor, and even exhibitor."

"Very well, but what is it you like to do best?"

"Editing. It is something very important and in a certain way definitive for the fate of the movie. It is commonly thought that editing a film consists of little more than handling a pair of scissors with some skill. It is much more than this because the editor has to interpret the story line and capture the director's idea so that the cinematographic story appears on the screen correctly narrated, and in addition with the rhythm and atmosphere appropriate to it. Two factors converge here: fluidity, the logic of the story; and the time span within which the different scenes elapse. The possibility also exists that there be changes of rhythm within the same work, as happens for example in a musical piece. Basically what is being attempted is to harmonize the tempo with the plot, and to construct the movie in such a way that its crescendos and its slow bridges form an esthetically valuable whole."

"Well, no wonder editing is important."

"So much so that the editor could spoil the best direction, and on the contrary he can rescue mediocre direction. As far as I'm concerned I almost always edit my films, or at least I collaborate in the task."

As Ismael Rodríguez talks of his films I think of all he has done for the Mexican cinema, both within and outside the country. Curiously, two facets can be distinguished in Rodríguez, one which triumphs or has triumphed in festivals and before foreign audiences, and another which still retains a great deal of popularity within Mexico. The first facet is the most recent one because it really consolidated itself in the decade of the sixties with *Hermanos de hierro* and above all *Animas Trujano.* * This has been one of the most honored films in our cinematic history, without forgetting *Tizoc,* which dates from 1956 and obtained a Silver Bear in Berlin, nor *Tierra de hombres* or *La cucaracha,* which represented us at Cannes in 1959.

Thinking of Ismael Rodríguez's second facet I ask him, "Who wrote the screenplay for *Nosotros los pobres?*"

"Pedro de Urdimalas and I. The previous screenplays of the same series, that is to say, *Ustedes los ricos* and *Pepe el toro,* I did myself; and I had *Ni pobres ni ricos* all ready to go when Pedro Infante died and the project had to be shelved."

"Tell me about Pedro Infante. Was he difficult to direct?"

"Not difficult really because he had an enormous talent for acting. He was one of the most versatile actors I have known. In the middle of shooting, after joking around, laughing his head off and pinching people, we would start shooting and right away he would cry if that's what the script called for. He mastered like no one else not only vocal expression but that of the gesture and the hands. He was a consummate artist in creating characters, and proof of that is the film *Los tres huastecos,* in which he appeared as a bandit, a priest, and a soldier. Infante had the necessary ability to render each of these figures identifiable to the spectator, in spite of the fact that he was all three at the same time and including one scene where they all appear without their respective costumes."

*Released in the United States as *The Important Man* [*Trans. note*]

"Could it be that you were the creator of Pedro Infante?"

"No. I would not claim that. At the most I would say that he developed at my side. He was singing at XEB and had had two or three small movie roles. I called him and I had faith in him. It is possible that some of my suggestions might have been useful to him."

"What kind of suggestions, for instance?"

"Well, for example, those that referred to Jorge Negrete. There was a natural propensity to compare these two actors but Jorge had the advantage, especially in voice quality. Pedro, by the way he handled himself, by gaining the audience's sympathy, and by charisma, managed to be his coactor's equal, as was very obvious in a film in which I used both of them called *Mano a mano.*"

"Was Infante very studious?"

"He was really intuitive. If you gave him a book to read, he'd get bored after a few pages. He preferred to have things explained to him, and he picked them up very quickly."

"You must have made a lot of money with *Nosotros los pobres,* isn't that true?"

"Yes. It was an extremely popular movie and it still is today even though I made it in 1947. You can be sure that it is the most-shown film in Mexico, without a doubt."

"More proof is provided by its appearance on TV."

"Of course, and you see that it has a large following. The atmosphere and the characters are essentially the same in the film version and the television version although Pedro Infante and Blanca Estela Pavón, who worked in the former, are gone. Nevertheless, as I was telling you, the story retains its values, and two very important figures replace those who disappeared. These two figures are Alberto Vázquez and Lupita Lara. There was considerable retouching of the story's idea because it was conformist in 1947. By this I mean that the poor looked upon their condition as very honorable and they were content with it in spite of the troubles they underwent. It was very difficult to become rich and they didn't even attempt it. But times have changed and that conformity would be out of tune with what the Mexican of 1973 thinks. Now the poor are poor but they try to better themselves, and this is what the television version portrays."

The Public's Sensitivity Changes

"Listen, *don* Ismael, I confess that I saw these movies when I was little and that I cried my eyes out when the little boy dies in the carpenter-shop fire, during the famous eye-gouging scene, and other similar ones. Now those same movies have been shown on television and my sons, of nineteen, eighteen, and nine years of age, break up laughing. I still cry but they laugh."

"Well, let me tell you, it is true that people's thinking has changed but here we have another kind of phenomenon. It isn't true that the film doesn't have an effect on them but that they fear ridicule. They receive the impression but instead of reacting to it in a normal way, which is tears, they do it in the opposite way, which is laughter. I'm not referring specifically to your sons but it is notorious that in the new generation there is much snobbishness . . . 'What will they think of me if I cry?' Faced with the doubt, they mask their tears with laughter."

"I think that violence might also play a part in this, that it has become our daily bread. If one sees violence everywhere and if every situation, dramatic or comic, is taken to its ultimate extreme, it is natural that sensibilities should be transformed. The strong scenes of years past instead of moving us now appear saccharine."

"I insist on the snobbishness hypothesis. We are very strong and very hard, and what might make us cry is kitsch."

"But *don* Ismael, isn't there a little bit of kitsch in these and other movies of that period?"

"Well, yes . . . It could be that they are slightly kitschy, no? But we have to keep in mind that they belong to the genre of melodrama and that melodrama has its characteristics, and is very respectable. There are good and bad melodramas, naturally."

Animas Trujano and the Prizes

"We have been talking," I tell Ismael Rodríguez, "of what could be called your Pedro Infante and Blanca Estela Pavón cycle; now I would like you to comment on movies of a different style, such as for example *Animas Trujano*, which is your best-known film outside the country.

"Well, I've always been interested in very diverse cinematic styles. I have also made international films. An example of this is *El niño y el muro,* which had nothing to do with Mexico. It deals with the problem of the two Germanies and was filmed partly in Czechoslovakia and partly in Spain . . . But you talk to me of *Animas Trujano.* You should have seen all the ribbing I had to put up with when I picked Toshiro Mifune to play the title role. Many people could not understand how a Japanese actor, however good he was, could play the role of a Mexican Indian. My critics did not realize that there are countrymen of ours, for example in Michoacán, who could pass for Japanese and that there are Japanese who look more Mexican than we do. The upshot was, you see, that I imported Mifune and everything came out very well."

"To the extent that *Animas Trujano* received many awards, like *María Candelaria.*"

"Yes. It obtained the Grand Prix from the San Francisco Film Festival and at the same time the award for best photography, which is Gabriel Figueroa's. It also won the Hollywood Foreign Press Association's Golden Globe and participated in the Venice Film Festival, or rather it didn't participate because it arrived late and was shown outside the festival."

"It might have received another prize."

"Perhaps, but we'll never know."

A Family of Cineasts

"You Rodríguez brothers constitute a family of cineasts. How long have you been in this business?"

"Actually, I would have to tell you a very long story. My father was a staunch Catholic and he got involved in the Cristero revolt. Things got pretty sticky and we had to expatriate ourselves. We landed in the United States where the old rebel opened up a bakery. My brother Roberto, who had always been very interested in photography, continued to study it, while José dedicated himself to matters of sound. He even invented an apparatus which, while it wasn't any big thing, was for those days quite interesting. We returned to Mexico around the year '30 or '31, in time to work on the filming of *Santa,* with Lupita Tovar, of the Nacional Productora de Películas. In that film the Rodríguez brothers were involved in sound matters and introduced their novel 'direct system.' "

While listening to Ismael Rodríguez I recall my reading of García Riera's book.* To tell the truth I haven't taken a survey, but, after all, the members of this illustrious clan have participated, in audio matters, in more than a hundred Mexican films.

"Was it more difficult to make movies in those days?"

"Yes. The technical aspect has come a long way and simplified things although, from another point of view, there have been new complications."

"And talking about the Mexican cinema, what difference do you find between the films made during the war and the present ones?"

"Well, in the last five or six years there have been changes that we could call radical. That's when this wave of somewhat daring or entirely pornographic neorealistic movies began. There is a tendency to inculcate in ourselves a certain European style but, in my judgment, we're not cut out for those things. There is something deep down that might be snobbishness, or whatever you want, but on seeing one of those films one tends to think that they took place in France or Sweden. In Mexico no, because we're different."

"Different in what sense?"

"Very simple. I don't like caviar—I prefer *chicharrón con molito.* And I'm not just being folksy. It is true of everybody in Mexico and what definitively differentiates us from other people."

"*Don* Ismael, to finish up, a question which I have asked other directors, such as for example Alejandro Galindo: why are there no new stars in our day?"

"There must be many reasons, some of which undoubtedly are impossible to analyze. Nonetheless there are others that can be pinpointed, as for example the existence of a con-

*Emilio García Riera, *Medio siglo de cine mexicano* (Mexico City: UNAM, 1968) [*Trans. note*]

tractual clause that prevents an artist from working exclusively with a particular producer or director for any length of time. As you know, I worked for many years with Blanca Estela Pavón and Pedro Infante, and I think that we all benefited. The actors, in these cases, have a chance to develop a style, instead of being the victims of vacillations and variations, and the director has the opportunity of gradually molding his artists to obtain from them, for mutual benefit, all the fruits of their talent."

And thus, in the midst of sound equipment and memories of the forties, I had to take my leave of Ismael Rodríguez, one of the builders of our Mexican cinema. One can accuse him of a certain Manicheism, as García Riera does in his very erudite and entertaining book, but one cannot deny him the great merit of depicting working-class neighborhoods without which, for example, Luis Alcoriza's *Mecánica nacional* would be unintelligible.

(photograph taken in early 1950s)

4

Luis Buñuel

"I have turned my back on everything! I am terribly pessimistic!"

The voice of Luis Buñuel seems to want to discourage me from going through with the interview. But I have to see him. Buñuel is one of the great figures of Mexican and world cinema, not only because of the quality of his films but also because of his status as a teacher. In a conversation with Alcoriza, and in another with Ripstein, the name of Buñuel came up repeatedly. It always comes up when people speak of films and innovation in cinematic art.

"But I am a misanthrope. I haven't granted interviews for a long time . . . Yes, of course, the newspapers write about me. In February, in Paris, Carlos Fuentes, a very good friend of mine, told me that the *New York Times* had asked him for an article on Buñuel. He asked me if it was all right with me. Of course it was; I have a great deal of confidence in him. But there are times when journalistic references are not exactly valid . . . Look here," Buñuel looks for a magazine and shows it to me. "This is a kind of Italian *Playboy.* It's called *Playman.* Well then, in this issue appears an article that claims to be an interview. But I never granted an interview to this gentleman who calls himself José Luis de Villalonga."

"Yes, I think I've heard of him. Isn't he part actor and part man-of-the-world, a member of the European jet set?"

Buñuel makes a motion with his hand which indicates more or less "it could be so." It is obvious that he cares little about it.

As it does every afternoon, it rains without fail. The atmosphere in this room of Buñuel's house becomes for that reason more comfortable. The espresso coffee he has offered me tastes more delicious. As we start to talk, *don* Luis's little dog pays me homage in the way that dogs do with visitors. She looks for a spot to lie down and begins to meditate very quietly.

"*Maestro,* I had a number of questions prepared. It's up to you whether I ask them or we simply converse."

"Let's hear the questions."

"What role does the cinema play in today's world? Just how efficient is it as a means of human expression and as a critical instrument?"

"It plays the same role as any other production of man's spirit. In this it is no different from the novel, theater, or painting. The cinema, it is true, does count on a somewhat larger public."

It is often the case, as I have felt at other times and I remember while listening to Buñuel, that the great creators are people of few words. They limit themselves to their work, which is the best way of not being limited. They act, do things, and don't feel the necessity to talk about them. Their actions speak for themselves, and they are perfect, authentic expressions. What could one ask Luis Buñuel that is not apparent from his films, from *The Andalusian Dog,* which dates from 1928, to *The Discreet Charm of the Bourgeoisie* from 1972? I begin to understand that the best interview with this great artist should consist, perhaps, in repeated viewings of the thirty films he has made. Buñuel is equivalent to his work. This man drinking coffee with me has said it all in his images and his stories.

"I note that there have been two easily distinguishable periods in the Mexican cinema. After a very auspicious beginning, albeit frustrated by technical deficiencies, our cinema dedicated itself to the task of entertaining the public. Of entertaining it in the most superficial sense. To give it a good time. But now a critical movement has begun. Now it is not a matter of presenting, for instance, the self-sacrificing Mexican mother with all the attributes we praise on May 10. There is a tendency to analyze that maternal figure and discover secret motivations. Perhaps some of those films' tear-jerking value will be lost, but we will gain in acuteness and veracity. And the public will be given opportunities for self-examination and rectification. Seeing ourselves as we really are we'll be able to improve ourselves morally and esthetically. At what time do you think that the cinema of Mexico assumed that critical function?"

"I don't even know if it has. And if so, I wouldn't know when it took on that role."

"Don't you think, *maestro,* that Mexico could produce a commercial cinema with artistic value which could also help somehow to rescue us from the sea of sham in which we are floundering?"

"It is possible that it could be possible . . . As far as it's being desirable . . . Anyway, it's all the same to me."

"But should the cinema always have a social value or does it fulfill its mission with a purely esthetic value? Or are the two values inseparable?"

"Over that I also don't lose any sleep."

Buñuel had told me he found himself "at the end of everything." And it is the truth. He is not excited by these matters. What really interests him is creation. And at this point the maker of *Viridiana* isn't even that excited over creating.

"For five years," he says, "they kept asking me to make *The Discreet Charm* . . . I didn't feel too motivated, but at last I agreed."

Another question: "What importance does surrealism have in contemporary cinema?"

"Surrealism has merged with life. Collages began many years ago, in advertising for example. In the cinema they are also used. There are no surrealist movies as such but there are some with elements of surrealism. It's the same thing that happens in poetry."

"Which of the movies you have made in Mexico do you think is the best?"

"I don't know. None. I have seen or seen again three or four. When I finish making them, I hand them over to the producer, he tells me 'okay,' and off I go. I don't know which one is the best or worst. The question is much discussed but since I don't go to the movies I don't know."

"Why don't you go to the movies?"

"I don't like crowds. I would watch movies if I were a Hollywood millionaire. Then I'd have a private screening room."

"*Maestro,* what value does plasticity have in the cinema? Could plasticity be sufficient to express everything that the cinema wishes?"

"Well, it should be at the service of the background. Plasticity is gratuitous when it doesn't express something, when it remains on the level of a merely visual symphony. It could be very good but the cinema based on it will not be complete. Form should not distract the spectator from the work's content. The film's moral should remain in sight without being concealed by ornamental details. Without background there is no possible cinema. Good or bad, the background has to be there."

"So, *maestro,* you rarely leave your house."

"No. I don't like to, and going out at night strikes me as horrible. I don't drive because of almost pathological attitudes I have toward people, toward traffic problems."

The rain keeps falling. The room becomes more shadowy. I reconstruct mentally Buñuel's biography since 1926 in Paris when he started out as a director's assistant with Jean Epstein in the film *Mauprat* and followed immediately with *The Fall of the House of Usher.* I would like to ask him about *The Andalusian Dog* and about Salvador Dalí, with whom he collaborated on the surrealistic short film. Some reminiscence about *L'Age d'Or* and his subsequent trip to Hollywood in the thirties during the heyday of American cinematography might be interesting.* And should I ask about the significance of *Los olvidados?* But one by one I reject these subjects. I can imag-

*The Young and the Damned [Trans. note]

Fernando Soler (middle) in Buñuel's *El gran calavera* (1949)

ine the answers: bare, terribly direct, or colored by an incurable skepticism.

But I don't believe that Buñuel is a skeptic even though he characterizes himself as such. Rather, he believes in very few things. The rest he does not care about because he has perceived the world's folly. He knows the backstage props and does not waste time with mere appearances. As far as genuine values are concerned, how can he not esteem them? Could a skeptic be as professional and prolific an artist as Luis Buñuel?

I am definitely not convinced of his skepticism. And regarding his misanthropy ...

"I am a misanthrope but I cease being one when I'm sharing a glass of wine with a couple of friends."

Now it is all clear. He is a misanthrope who believes in friendship and celebrates it with the simplicity and efficacy of one of the oldest and noblest rituals: drinking a glass of wine. I imagine such a scene in this very room. Could Alcoriza be one of the group?

"Alcoriza," says Buñuel, "is an intimate friend of mine. He saw Europe through my eyes. This, of course, doesn't mean anything. He has his own personality and talent."

Yes, it is possible that Alcoriza, and perhaps Ripstein, get together with Buñuel. Carlos Fuentes, Ripstein, and Alatriste recognize in him the most genuine and rigorous of teachers.

Perhaps the trait of rigor is the one that best characterizes Buñuel. It is possible that rigor is the key to understanding him —a rigor that should be understood as lucid intelligence. It is said that mathematics is a rigorous discipline because it leaves nothing to chance. Nothing is left unfinished, everything acquires a neat, clear, and distinct form. Rigor consists of disregarding trifles and useless data. And this is what Buñuel does in his art and in his life. They are constructions of geometric exactness in which all vacillation is eliminated. However, they are not cold forms. They make a vivid distinction between the wheat and the chaff.

It is like when Buñuel was telling me he was a misanthrope while at the same time naming his friends. On the one hand, people horrify him and are not worth a penny to him; but on the other, there are human beings with whom he talks and who understand him—his friends, his true friends.

Cranky and sharp-tongued, Buñuel is a good and generous man in spite of having very few beliefs. Generous and shrewd, he is a friend of the truth above all, although he knows that truth tends to be concealed behind masks and words.

When we have finished our coffee, after I don't know how much time, perhaps two hours, he solicitously accompanies me to the door; he protects himself with the light sweater he wears and brings me a newspaper to cover my head with ... I shouldn't get wet and catch a cold.

5

 **Luis Alcoriza**

"I really liked *Mecánica nacional.* Congratulations. At last vulgarity is attacked from its very source."

Luis Alcoriza receives my words without expression. We are in the living room of his home, in the suburb of Narvarte, and I cannot say that he welcomed me with great pleasure. He dislikes interviews. An enemy of rhetoric, he prefers to make movies rather than talk about them.

"Well, yes," he finally answers, "*Mecánica nacional* reflects the sentimentality typical of the Mexican people. Generally it is a canvas of sorts on which I tried to picture people's customs. Those people one sees at all times, everywhere. You'll remember from that movie the pair of Spanish kids, very sportily dressed, who dedicate themselves relentlessly to eating. They are not gratuitous types, they represent the vestiges of the 'honorable Spanish colony,' which maintains its gastronomic patriotism no matter what."

"I like the way you have your books," I say to break the ice. "All of these books are heavily worn. One can tell that you have read them and that they aren't solely for adornment."

"Well, that is the way it should be ... Of course there are books for reference only, and these aren't used as much."

"But all intellectual labors should be that—labor—don't you think? I say it because there is also intellectual posturing which doesn't go deeply into anything and results simply in lining up books on the shelves, without opening them. *Mecánica nacional* takes for granted much reflection, reading, and observation, although it does not make them obvious. It is not a movie that displays its intellectual origins. On the other hand there are others like *Patsy mi amor* that try at all costs, say by means of a desperately slow pace, to demonstrate that they have a very refined origin."

Alcoriza lets me talk. He has a poker face. He neither agrees nor disagrees.

"I think that being an intellectual is the same as being a carpenter," he points out in a very polite voice. "That is to say, one has a job, a profession, and with them one works and accomplishes things; but it is man who does these things, and he should behave and express himself as such. As to the intellectual who functions only within the boundaries of his readings and meditation and who doesn't abandon his attitude ..."

"Such a limited intellectual at times can be very sterile."

"Listen, since the twenties, since the good old days of surrealism, from what I have read and from my discussions with Buñuel, I know that the word 'intellectual' was already being used in a pejorative sense."

Portrait of Luis Buñuel

"Now that you mention Buñuel, has he meant much in your career?"

"Everything, but not exclusively in the cinema. As a friend and teacher, Buñuel is one of the most important figures in my life. He is present even in small actions that nevertheless bring us closer together, like the act of knowing a wine. For me it's an ethical barrier. When I think of him, and without his even being aware of it, he acts like a brake, like a moral force that determines my conduct."

"How long have you known Luis Buñuel?"

"Since the year we started working together, which was '49. I had seen him before, knew who he was, but I didn't meet him until then."

"And what was that relationship like? Weren't there difficulties in the beginning? Because to me Buñuel doesn't seem to be too accessible, isn't that true?"

"Buñuel is one of the most good and noble men in existence."

"Well, yes, but difficult . . ."

"No, no, no . . . That is to say, we are both impassioned and argue a lot, and this is all due to temperament. But my relationship with him was not difficult. No, because I immediately let down my guard. At our first meeting, I attached myself to him like an octopus to extract everything he could and did give me, and continues giving me. With me that contact with Luis, that contact which is renewed every time he returns to Mexico after one of his absences, is like a total reawakening. We talk and he strengthens me and at times we strengthen each other."

"As a person he must be sensational."

"Sensational as a person and in every other way, because he also cannot be classified as a film director. Buñuel is a great poet, and a black poet besides, one of the good ones; and a satiric thinker who expresses himself with the cinematic image instead of the written word. Because of that he maintains himself. Because he is by autonomasia the man of ideas, the man of mystery (but these words are really not taken seriously) . . . Buñuel is the man who always discovers something and is always giving us something new. And for that it is not necessary for him to change his technique. He doesn't worry in the slightest over these things. With the greatest ease he fills us with ideas and freshness, and liberates us."

"Buñuel still has not made an impression on the average Mexican, true?"

"A big one on young people."

"But, on the other hand, the usual moviegoer who queues up on Saturdays or Sundays . . ."

"Because it is a public that has let itself be dulled by the cinema of consumerism. The cinema entails this danger, perhaps in the same form as other artistic expression. I don't know if the same thing is happening with novels, but I guess so; people prefer things that will entertain them, and what causes thinking makes them a little lazy. A Buñuel film always sets one to thinking. The spectator cannot remain in his seat as a simple recipient. He has to collaborate with the creator."

From Scriptwriter and Actor to Film Director

Luis Alcoriza's career in Mexican films began far from the megaphone. He acted in many films of the forties, and many people now would be surprised if *María Magdalena* and *Reina de reinas* were to be exhibited again and they saw him play Jesus of Nazareth. He also worked in a 1943 version of *Naná*, which starred Lupe Vélez, and in another—I throw out examples at random—called *Flor de caña* with María Antonieta Pons. By that time he was writing scripts. This was precisely why he came to know Luis Buñuel.

"In 1949," Alcoriza reminisces, "I wrote with him the script for *Los olvidados,* which was the first film we made together. The last one was *El ángel exterminador,* which marks our professional separation because from that point on I dedicated myself to directing. I became a director in a roundabout way, as you can see. This was caused by various factors."

"Before going on, it is interesting to note your wife's collaboration with you in your work as a screenwriter. Is it true you have worked together a lot?"

"Very much. My wife and I wrote I don't know how many scripts and adaptations."

"And how long have you been involved in the artistic milieu?"

"Always, since I was a kid. My first appearance on a stage was in the arms of my mother, who was the lead actress. My father was the company's director and empresario. So you see, except for the time I spent in school, everything else has been in the theater. We toured all over Spain and the Spanish possessions in Africa; then came the war and, well, you know the story."

Alcoriza tells me many things in a broad, spotty, and disorganized dialogue, as if this weren't an interview. He says that he began writing for the theater and not films, and that those

A scene from *Mecánica nacional*

pieces were very bad. He refers to some of his old movies like *El inocente* with Silvia Pinal and Pedro Infante, and *Tarahumara* and *Tlayucan* (made in 1961), which, according to him, anticipates *Mecánica nacional.*

A New Mexican Cinema Does Not Exist

"Could you tell me about the new Mexican cinema?" I ask Alcoriza.

"Certainly, I can talk about that and many other things. In the first place, that business about a new Mexican cinema . . . There are young directors, very cultured, very talented, thoroughly professional . . . There are favorable conditions; for example, censorship is being relaxed, as is evident to all of us. There are many opportunities, but all this does not constitute proof of the existence of a movement that could be called new cinema. I think of Brazil's, which was based on a solidly constituted group whose members defended political ideas and in the process exposed themselves to persecution and other troubles. It was a movement that encompassed all the requirements of the cinema as a medium of communication, that is to say, there were directors and actors involved in it, they could count on people to distribute and exhibit their films, and in addition they arranged for their own financing. In what we call the new Mexican cinema none of these conditions are present. In it participate a group of good friends who get along very well, but that is all."

"I think that the Mexican cinema, for reasons attributable to our national character, is one of the most individualistic and least homogeneous . . ."

"Exactly, our cinema seems to lack a collective spirit. Everyone goes his own way and does what he feels like doing. What is called new Mexican cinema is restricted to one important development, but that one may not be important enough to compare to the Brazilian cinema. This development consists in the making of more ambitious films, more polished and expensive. The new directors have freed themselves from the restrictions that held back previous generations. They have liberated themselves a little, for example, from the dependence on 'stars' and from the dependence on a budget—both very broad areas in which there is now much greater freedom. Today a young director can arrive at Churubusco with a script in hand and obtain money to make it. This is the situation of Arau, it is the situation of Ripstein and of Alberto Isaac. What has happened is that now a director's talent and prestige are financed, and he is no longer, as in the past, an individual who is hired to direct an existing script and who arrives on the set literally surrounded by all kinds of limitations."

"Then it could be said that films are really the director's?"

"Yes, yes, of course."

"And this matter about censorship being eased should also be important; but I still doubt that this softening is real and that censorship will eventually disappear."

"Disappear—no! I don't know about the future. I couldn't say."

"For example, was *Mecánica nacional* cut very much?"

"Nothing—not even one frame. And it is probable that at some other time that movie wouldn't have been passed. I note that if we compare two eras—that in which I started out in the movies and the present one—we can see that a good deal more freedom exists now. Before, the producer decided everything. If you weren't lucky enough to convince one of those gentlemen to make a film—and I can't complain because I was lucky —the doors were shut. The producer could say that he wanted the picture in three weeks, and that was terrible, but there were directors who accepted it because they had families to feed and, in a word, responsibilities."

"Were conditions of that kind imposed on you?"

"It was tried, but I never accepted them. I weathered the economic storms as best I could . . . And now on the other hand, as I was telling you, very important and costly films are being planned that directors propose directly to Churubusco and the Cinematographic Bank. And not only are they planned but also made. We have just mentioned Alberto Isaac and Alfonso Arau, and they are two good examples of what I'm talking about. There is a coproduction system in which the director participates directly, cooperatives are formed, artists are gathered, etc."

"And there are also new producers, right?"

"Yes, Escorpio is a new company, as are Marco Polo and Alfa Centauri. Actually there are a number, and I think that slightly better movies have been made."

Alcoriza has offered me an excellent cup of coffee, which is doubly welcome because outside it is raining and cold.

"Well then, how is the Mexican cinema doing in comparison with other countries?"

"Bad, frankly. We have many obstacles, one of which is censorship. I have just said that it has softened, but this doesn't mean it has disappeared. And anyway, censorship is not only official. In this respect undue blame is cast on Hiram García Borja, and this is unjust. I think that the fault lies basically with the public, which is not ready, which is a public addicted to *fotonovelas,* to Pepines and all those things. A public that doesn't read and is at the mercy of parents' societies and moralistic organizations of all kinds."

"Yes, I've been told that in the provinces these organizations are very powerful."

"And here in the capital, too. They exert pressure on the Dirección de Cinematografía and on the people. They insist that such and such a thing not be exhibited and they prevent the public from enjoying itself and filmmakers from working without impediments. These societies are the ones that cause harm and which hinder us. You must have read this constantly: 'This movie is not fit for children, it is unsuitable, it is offensive ...' As you can see it is not only official censorship that has restrained us."

"It is prudishness."

"It is the prudishness of the people, the moralists, and so forth. And definitely the outcome is that we cannot make the films that are made in the United States, in Italy, or in France. The situation is not just confined to Mexico. In Colombia, where censorship practically didn't exist, *Last Tango in Paris* has provoked a fierce reaction, and now there is censorship, and very tight at that."

"Very well, but prudishness has another defect: it leads to cheapness."

"Not necessarily. Notice how the people who have seen *Last Tango* ... or at least a good part of them, instead of appreciating Bertolucci's work have been fascinated by the scene with the butter. That is to say that even if there were complete freedom bad taste would still be bad taste, and the most that one could aspire to under these conditions would be pornography. Now then, if I had a choice I would choose the latter in place of the saccharine pastries that are served up to the public."

The Cinema Has Idiotized Us

"You're very much interested in Mexico, aren't you? The reactions of our people interest you. Children interest you. Like, for example, those infantile faces that appear in *Esperanza* ... The other day in the studios I saw that film of yours which is part of *Fe, esperanza y caridad.* The sound was being rerecorded ... Well, I was saying that one scene consists of children's faces. They are fascinated by a horrible scene: a serpent devouring a rabbit. Were you interested in that innocence, that childish impassiveness?"

"What interested me was the cruelty of those children. They were delighted, they didn't miss one detail of the rabbit's sacrifice. They weren't even distracted by the lights. They only had eyes for the serpent and its victim. The child is a fighting animal. They come into the world endowed with great egoism and ferocity. They want to survive and struggle, and sentimental considerations do not deter them. This is a child, and what do we make of him? Well, an imbecile. We fill his head with nonsense until we manage to create a perfect castrated male. We call them 'honest' and 'useful' men. As children we have all been told that. That is what we have to be. But basically what is being accomplished is the subjection of those young people. To mold them in such a way that they will allow themselves to be crushed without resistance. They are idiotized. They are limited and entranced ... I assure you that I am not at all happy with this world of ours, and I do everything possible to combat it. Returning to our subject of the cinema, I believe that the majority of the films made have one fundamental objective: to prevent people from seeing the imperfections of the society in which they live. To me it seems that the purposes of art are at precisely the opposite pole. Art should illuminate and not conceal."

"Isn't there something of misogyny in your films?"

"No one could be less misogynistic than I. Why do you ask me that?"

"But you make fun of motherhood, of the devout ...."

"Let's understand each other. I mock symbols. I think it is very legitimate to love one's own mother. I loved mine very much, but this has nothing to do with Mother with a capital 'M.' What terrifies me—I repeat—are symbols: of Mother, of Father ... The taboos, the authorities, respect for everything. I am convinced that the human being does not have the texture we have insisted on seeing in him. He is something else, very different from what we were told. Now we are discovering it and we are beginning to be terrified, really to terrify

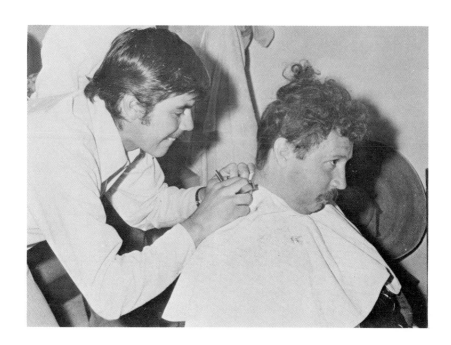

Luis Alcoriza shooting *Las fuerzas vivas* on location in Querétaro

ourselves when we contemplate our true selves. Our astonish-
ment has made us violent. We haven't thought of anything else
to destroy. We assail the world and ourselves. We have fallen
into a horrendous savagery, a product more of stupidity than
cruelty. This is the bad thing: that stupidity should be the basis
of it all . . . Because cruelty, if one takes a good look at it, is
comprehensible. If a sadist finds pleasure in the suffering of
others it is natural that he should act like a sadist. This I can
understand. But stupid cruelty is unintelligible, and it happens
all the time. It is kicking a dog in one's path, a defenseless dog,
asleep and perhaps ill. From this to burning children with
napalm is not a big step. There is a very logical sequence that
is easily developed. Extermination in gas chambers is not
something so very distant from us . . . I tell you, things are bad.
As Sartre said in a magnificent prologue: 'The bad thing is not
that man does these things but that he is always willing to do
them again!' "

Seeking Success and Money

"Then," I interrupt Alcoriza, "what the cinema does, and
what television, literature, and the rest of the mass media, as
they are now called, do is present us the world as it is not."
"Of course, of course . . . And diligently seek success and
money."
"Another sickness of our times?"
"It was one of the great things that Buñuel taught me: the
total disregard for money. I really don't know whether to be
thankful for this or to be furious with him," Alcoriza smiles
while saying this, "but the fact is that this is the way I think.
We are corroded by commercialism. And everything is fouled
by it. They would have us believe that we live in the best of
all possible worlds, but it's only a stupid pretense. Ingenuous
souls might fall into that. Not we, who are sincerely terrified,
as I was telling you a moment ago."
"And such frankness bothers many people, don't you think?"
"And we are not saying a millionth part of what should be
said. In other countries the outcry is stronger, while in ours it
is barely a whimper."

"In what countries is the outcry sharpest? In France? In the United States?"

"At least there is greater liberty in those countries . . . the possibility of speaking out. But everywhere—and don't you doubt it—the cineast is held down. He has to bend before determined pressures . . . There are some who escape genially, like Buñuel, who says what he wishes in an elegant way, and no one can talk back to him and the entire world admires him."

"But isn't the field widening every day?"

"I don't know. There are tremendous limitations. It isn't the same as writing a novel, for which the only thing you need is a scrap of paper . . . To make movies capital is required, and this capital naturally is someone else's. And that someone else does not wish to risk it, apart from the possibility that he won't see eye to eye with the cineast whose thinking is so unstructured."

"There is something of puritanism . . ."

"Certainly, people are afraid of known things. They don't want to recognize a certain ugliness."

"I had an experience in my sons' school. Someone suggested showing films on drug addicts. Not strong films, but impressive ones; of hospitals and all those things. But the parents opposed it and in general everyone else in a position to express an opinion."

"It's what we were saying: The fear of confronting reality. It is puritan morality, which condemns the sin but more energetically condemns the publicity concerning it. It's all right to commit the acts but what cannot be tolerated is their discussion . . ."

"But people are frightened of seeing things in a theater. In a magazine, in a book . . . it isn't as serious. But in the movies . . ."

Power and the Risk of the Image

"Of course," responds the cineast. "It is that the image is brutal, you know. With the image one has to proceed with great caution, and use esthetic, not moral, scruples. It has happened to me a number of times . . . What you write or what you read in a book may be very daring, or whatever, but at the same time it is capable of attaining beauty. The word can excite the reader's imagination but it does not present objects in their innate brutality . . . I don't know if I make myself clear. There is a difference between talking about something and showing it. The first is a more indirect procedure. The second has an immediate effect. There is no in-between. The thing is there . . ."

"I understand."

Alcoriza is an aggressive personage, yet he is full of common sense. He has given me a good lesson in it as well as in intellectual vigor and honesty, even though he dislikes the word. After saying good-bye to him, and while rolling down my car window, I thought of what he had said. In his cry of protest and his rebellion against symbols. In his preaching in favor of lack of respect. I thought also of Buñuel. And I thought of Raquel Rojas, with whom he has maintained a model marriage for many years. A lack of respect? Yes, but toward symbols, not toward genuine sentiments, or obligations freely assumed. This seems to be the key of the new morality. I know that I came not to discuss morality but the cinema; but it would be incorrect to differentiate between the two. What is behind all artistic activity but a great moral impulse? At least that is what there should be, especially when art is a mass art, when it reaches so many people and powerfully influences their thinking and their conduct.

6

Felipe Cazals

Felipe Cazals. Thirty-three years old, mustachioed, very intelligent and sure of himself. His filmography is not yet very extensive but there are those who complain that it has been the most expensive. It is worthwhile to list it in full: it started with short films among which the following stand out—*¡Que se callen!,* filmed in 1965, which tells the story of León Felipe;* *El sortilegio irónico* in the same year; *Cartas de Mariana Alcoforado,* 1966; *La otra guerra,* 1967; and *Trabajos olímpicos,* 1968. That same year he made his first full-length motion picture, *La manzana de la discordia.* He undertook *Familiaridades* in 1969, *Emiliano Zapata* in 1970, and *El jardín de tía Isabel* in 1971. His most recent picture is *Aquellos años,* made in 1972.

Cazals receives me in his extremely elegant Churubusco

*León Felipe Camino (1884–1968), Spanish postmodernist poet. Left Spain after Civil War and continued his career in South America and Mexico [*Trans. note*].

office. While we talk he drinks a couple of beers. The conversation is rapid, and on very concrete subjects. More than a dialogue, it constitutes a series of memorandums by Cazals. It is better to transcribe them in this form, almost as aphorisms. As flashes.

On Cinematographic Creation

"The response," Cazals points out, "might seem impudent and also presumptuous, but it is the only one I could give you: to make film is to enjoy it. I don't know if you understand what I'm trying to say. It is enjoyment in the most precise and broadest meaning of that word. It is to vent a passion, and that's why I do it, that is to say, I am a cineast out of passion. On this is also based my perpetual conflict with the industry because, if the cinema's original sin is that of being an industrial product, this same circumstance confronts it with passion. It renders it contradictory from its origin."

The Cinema As Adventure

"I would like to be filming twenty-four hours a day. Filming everything filmable. And essentially that's what I do. Right now I find myself in the middle of filming. And it's because the cinema is this century's last adventure. If science in the final analysis is nothing more than the explanation of what we don't know, art is the re-creation of same. It is the re-creation of the unknown. Any creator has before him the infinite possibility of inventing everything. Very well then, the cineast is the only creator requiring enormous resources and is therefore placed in the center of a great technical and financial apparatus. Luckily for him, there are not yet computers or electronic systems that can replace him. The film director is the captain of this last adventure because he is indispensable and at the same time unforeseeable. In the face of technology this is our only strength."

Industrial Interests and Artistic Ones

"On the one hand the binomial formed by industry and financiers, and on the other the cineast's intentions of expressing something very personal truly represent a problem. To resolve it there is only one formula: learn to dish it out. No more, no less. One learns to feint, to lie, to smile, to deceive, to have false modesty, to allow oneself to be deceived, to throw oneself out the window when they think you wouldn't do it ... It is like the *commedia dell'arte.*"

Everyone Tries to Do Things Well

"I made two films outside the industry: *La manzana de la discordia* and *Familiaridades,* within the industry, to my eternal shame, *Emiliano Zapata.* I paid my dues for joining the Sección de Directores; and if I am to be sincere I'll tell you that I never intended to make a bad film. I don't think anyone would deliberately do something badly. For example, I suppose the people who write certain soap operas try to do the best they can ...

"I don't know if in this case a certain defense mechanism is functioning which I turn on so as not to commit suicide, but I insist that I worked on *Zapata* with the best intentions under the circumstances that surrounded me.

"It isn't necessary to condemn reputedly commercial directors," he continues. "The severity with which they are at times judged has to be tempered. They were salaried directors; something like agents. From the year '47 or between '50 and '60, one has to recognize that the Mexican cinema suffered from a severe lack of resources. The producers had the mentality of ladder salesmen on Sundays. Only the latent illiteracy of Mexicans made possible the continued functioning of that cinema.

"There are already hopeful signs: Cantinflas's last few films are in the exact style of the fifties, and their drop in popularity has been notorious. This loss is directly related to the reduction of illiteracy. If within five years no one goes to these movies

A scene from *Canoa*

anymore it will be a magnificent sign. If even in Tingüindín they fail to attract a public it will mean the country's culture has progressed.

"The primordial misery of Mexico relates to culture, and fortunately that misery is disappearing."

What the New Cinema Signifies

"Certain producers once told us: 'Make your little cinema, win prizes, but in the final analysis we will still be the pillars of the industry. After two years we continued winning prizes as it were, but the industry supports itself on our work in spite of all the emissaries of the past growling in their caves.

"Let's not talk of a new cinema. Let's talk of the contemporary cinema. I am opposed to that term, which sounds petty bourgeois to me and in which I sense a class and clique spirit. The contemporary cinema, the one being made, is a reality, and, most important, it is an irreversible reality. After the worst picture any of us make, no melodrama of the previous decade will be successful, and no producer will dare make one."

Carlos Fuentes and *Aquellos años*

"Working with Carlos Fuentes in *Aquellos años* was stupendous. It left me with very good memories. Carlos worked for three months on his own as I did for three. Later we got together and we worked another nine months, of which two passed without our being able to agree on anything while the next three were quite pleasant—we decided that everything could be ironed out around a table—and the last four were characterized by a total affinity. They made it possible for me to establish a stupendous friendship with Fuentes. One of my upcoming pictures—I am working on it now—which was not adapted by Carlos, so you can see how well we understand each other, is *Las buenas conciencias.*"

Some Biographical Data

"My life story is infinite, and if a journey starting from my navel is proposed, I am delighted ...

"Well, I'll tell you, after getting expelled from the Liceo Franco Mexicano I sported boots and a sabre: I spent a few years in the Latin American Military Academy, which stimulated in me a dictatorial streak I still have. While I was there, my mother discovered that my moral and religious inclinations left much to be desired; and then I entered medical school, a fertile seeding-ground where I had all kinds of friends—businessmen, politicians, etc. I studied medicine for a year, and luckily I realized that I had nothing to contribute to that profession. I got into the Hippodrome out of vagrancy. I exercised horses and was a proxy jockey. I experienced typical middle-class guilt pangs and audited classes at the University. In this way I got to know the cinema clubs and I let myself get involved by those games of artifice that are Griffith, Fritz Lang, etc. I obtained a scholarship to IDEC in Paris for three years. I was an assistant director, I was in France, Italy, and Spain; and I returned to begin anew, to climb the ladder like everyone else. Perhaps with a little more luck but nothing extraordinary."

Commercial and Artistic Feelings

"It is practically impossible to reconcile commercial with artistic interests. The reason for this is one of meridian clarity: the creative process, in any field, depends on a seizure of conscience, a surrender, and a risk for the creator. Once the creation is completed, the product is converted into a cadaver. It no longer has any meaning for the artist because it belongs to the spectators. If the product is well made the spectator will make an effort and will understand it. But in the cinema there is the idea that things turn out exactly inversely: 'The picture is made to appeal to the public.' Then later the artistic part is subdued beforehand by the auditory, wherefore the creative level is subordinated to industrial, economic, and other exigencies. There are exceptions to the rule, like a Bergman film, *Cries and Whispers,* which I have just seen. It is the most commercial yet the most perfect of its author's. It follows his lineaments of searching, his attitude of inexorable analysis of himself and his own creative capacities.

"And I tell you, it is also the most commercial," Cazals repeats forcefully.

Everyone Wants to Make Cinema

"Yes, everyone wants to make cinema. Because of its being a fad, the desire for fame, and more than ever the tendency toward stardom. In Mexico if everybody who wants to be a cineast had wings, we wouldn't be able to see the sun.

"The cinema industry has always been susceptible to bluff. It is an industry that moves only one hundred fifty million

A scene from *Aquellos años*

pesos a year, in a revolving fund, and which nevertheless takes up entire pages in newspapers, and has sections devoted to it. Tell me what industry, however important it may be, has such public resonance.

"As I say, no one is indifferent to the cinema, and they all cherish the secret desire to be new Fellinis."

Cinema of Spectators and Not Consumers

"The road that the Mexican cinema should follow is that of quality in every respect. And also quantity because it is vital that production increase. But we need more enthusiasm, better distribution ...

"But the most important part of the industry is its manpower. In a developing country like ours, people qualified in diverse activities are necessary. The cinema is no exception, and often technicians and others have to be imported from abroad.

"Thousands of people work at all levels, in every area. This is indispensable and all to the good, as long as the director's supreme authority is maintained.

"In the history of the Mexican cinema our generation is a bridge, and for that reason its responsibility is great. We came into an established organization and our mission consists in shattering it. This is what we are trying to do. Those who follow us won't find things as they are now. For example, even now when a director is given an assignment he is told: 'You have such and such an amount of money, so many days, and the picture must contain these ingredients.' The director accepts so he can work. But we are infiltrating our point of view. Soon the old criteria will no longer be valid. As I told you a moment ago, the director has to establish himself in the greatest authority.

"In this way we shall be moving toward a new conception of the cinema. It will no longer be for a consumer, as it is now, but for a genuine spectator. At the moment, the confusion between consumer and spectator is the gravest problem in relation to the destiny of filmmaking. People who go to movies are ruminant beings who eat popcorn. The spectator of the future will really go to see a picture and to participate in it as all men participate when they come face to face with a work of art."

7

Salomón Laiter

"The crisis we are seeing in the Mexican cinema is nothing more than a part of the worldwide crisis which is affecting the filmmaking industry. It consists of a series of both cultural and technical problems—of all kinds. And the industry has to resolve them all if it wants to survive."

Salomón Laiter had greeted me in his study, which had brown leather chairs and wall-to-wall yellow and white carpeting. It is an open room, conducive to conversation and discussion.

"We're getting sidetracked. How did you get into this world —one so full of conflicts, hopes, and frustrations?"

"It's been seventeen years since I started. You see, I was a high school student, and I used to play hooky and go to the movies. Once I saw *Los olvidados,* by Buñuel, and thought to myself that it was truly *the* work of our times. Through the language that Buñuel used, he spoke of things that mattered to us. It was authentic art—our art—one which I as a person could practice; one which I could give myself up to. Since that time, I've worked in the movie industry, even though my work hasn't always been up front. I've read, thought, written . . . I've done a lot of things which led into cinematography."

The director of *Las puertas del paraíso* is young. I'd guess that he's over thirty but under forty years of age. He speaks like many intellectuals, with precision. He doesn't hesitate when choosing words, and those he uses almost always—and very effectively—indicate what he means.

"Is the present Mexican cinema bad?"

"I won't deny it, but one cannot make a condemnatory judgment without qualifying it. As I told you a minute ago, our industry is involved in a crisis which is also affecting the North American, French, British, Italian, even the German cinema. Here in Mexico there have been some very important figures —people of worldwide importance, and we can't ignore them. But we are now in a new era, a very hard one. It demands from all of us an attitude which until now has not been evident, either with relation to cinematic works, or with relation to the audience at which the work is directed."

"I've heard talk of labor conflicts which slow down production."

"I have too, but these conflicts, in spite of the fact that they can be very bothersome for cineasts, are not the cause of the crisis. The crisis, you can be sure, comes from other sources."

"From bad writers?"

To Leave Behind the Good Ones: A Sign of Underdevelopment

"That is another factor. It's true that we don't have any really good writers within the industry, with some exceptions. I think that there exists a sort of indifference on the part of the people who truly could contribute to the industry by writing. One wonders—where are the Juan García Ponces, the Ibargüengoitias . . . ? And we can think not only of writers. For example, consider Juan José Gurrola. With what he did in theater and with the talent he showed, we could be sure that he ought to contribute to movies. Why doesn't he?"

"The same with Usigli."

"Of course."

"It's as if being a specialist, or excelling in one area, results in closing the doors to it. It's a paradoxical situation, don't you think?"

"I think," answered Laiter, "that it's only a characteristic of underdevelopment. You see the system in everyone, nowhere more than in the film industry."

Digression about Painting

"Well and good, but we agree that the Mexican cinema has been important. Why has this lessened? I have the impression that in one era—say that of El Indio Fernández and Julio Bracho—it was more important than our literature, and on a par with our painting. That is, it was an art intimately connected to reality, aware of its resources, and very able to express what was then interesting."

"Will you allow me to digress? I don't think that Mexican painting—and I'm referring to muralism—has ever reached the level of painting in other countries. As an indicator of a circumstance and a problem, it's been as ineffective as Russian social painting. Do I make myself clear?"

"Let's not get into that. I return to my question: why has the old impulse been lost?"

People Are Not Going to Movies

"And I return to my initial answer: we can't ask this only with reference to our cinema, but we have to consider that of the entire world. Look, I just returned from Germany: there I saw empty theaters. In 90 percent of them they were showing pornographic films, and they were still empty. There were usually five or ten young Luftwaffe men in them and that was it. People are not going to movies. They prefer to stay at home, which can probably be explained by the fact that television offers the same fare as the theater. But it's free, and there's no personal risk involved. The point is this: how do you ask, for example, a New Yorker, to leave his home and go out on the street when there's a chance of being shot in any of five or six spots along the way. All this simply to see something familiar which doesn't add anything to his knowledge? Because large cities like New York—and here I'll digress again—are subject these days to all the anguish and violence which contemporary problems have unleashed, how do you ask people to leave home, and cause their family and friends endless worry?"

"It is, of course, a terrible situation."

A Crisis That Could Save Us

"Don't think that way. It's not terrible. I think that it's beneficial. Do you know what will come of all this? A new cinema: a cinema that may be conceived as a real work of art, as an authentic and original creation quite apart from the star system and ego problems that besiege us today. For a society like the one we've made in the second half of the twentieth century—tied to consumerism, humiliated by advertising, abandoned and alone—the film industry has to provide an answer. And this answer is found in true art. Forty years ago Artaud said that art is the cell that regenerates the social organism; that's how it has to be seen. To think of the cinema this way is to leave behind our archaic modes of behavior."

"Do you think that there are either stars or monsters that are sacred cows?"

"There shouldn't be. Hollywood has definitely ended the era of glamour, and this is true for the rest of the world cinema. Moviemaking is an art, and one has to approach it with all the austerity that art demands. Moreover, it is a technique, and it is necessary to master the technique, to become a good official, that is, a person who masters the material secrets, great and small. It is also work involving equipment; but this does not mean that the director is the sole creator of the film. He's the coordinator, the one responsible ... anything you wish, but behind him is the work—the ideas and methods—of many other persons."

"You talk about austerity, and yet the cinema is one of the least austere activities that exists. One has only to think about the money those who dedicate themselves to the cinema can make."

"That's another illusion which used to be valid but which is now without basis. In Hollywood they pay stars the minimum salaries; here, too."

Megalomania, a Sterile Sin

"You have also mentioned megalomania. I think that artists cannot avoid a certain amount of pride, a certain amount of vanity."

"Well, they should. I remember once an Italian cineast told me his impressions about this problem. An actor from our cinema arrived in Rome. This man, the Italian told me, stayed in his hotel to await the arrival of the reporters. The Italian smiled. He didn't realize, he added, that we're not geniuses. We're artisans, the makers of a work that we ought to see humbly. Newspapermen will come and do interviews and plot stories, but they too are craftsmen. Reporters also do their job."

"Okay, I think your Italian friend was right."

"Of course he was. Can you tell me what kind of satisfaction you get from seeing our name in the pages of a newspaper if these pages are paid for, and if what is written about us simply comes off an assembly line?"

Why Are Movies Made Today?

"I agree. And I think your stance is the most honorable and conscientious one. But, tell me, why then are movies made?"

"Filmmaking is an industry. It's a source of jobs, a modus vivendi for a lot of people, and as such one has to respect and understand it. But it's also an art, and to speak of it in these terms—that is, at the artistic level—I return to what Artaud said. It is a regenerating cell. It's the point of origin of new and healthy formations inside the social body. It is a source of authenticity and true humanity. This is all the more apparent because the present world is being dehumanized. Science and technology are drowning and draining us. Did you see recently that the Nobel Prize winner—the one who invented transistors—very seriously proposed to the feeble minded to consent to sterilization? And not only the feeble minded but also individuals with IQs of 90 to 100. This is very serious. We're in the dawn of an age in which, because of surgery and drugs, it will be possible to regulate our emotions and standardize our characters. Man has never suffered such strong assaults—and art should act to free him. It ought to begin the task of regeneration. It ought to constitute Artaud's cell—which begins a new being, free of disease, over the base of the ruined and corroded old one. This is the mission of the cinema. Those who prefer vanity to collaboration in this business have chosen the wrong path."

"Vanity then is not inherent in the artist?"

"I think that every day of his life on awaking Picasso asked himself if his painting was really valuable. There does not exist a true artist vain enough to feel satisfied. As far as someone thinking that he's already done it all, that he already *is*, or that he's already arrived at the end of the road—when he thinks that, he's finished. At that moment he ceases to have any use for art."

"Then, when the cinema has become young again and abandoned its aspirations to glamour, to pomp and circumstance, people will leave their homes, even in New York, to go see a good movie."

"That's how it should be. Because movies don't stupidly repeat what is on television. They will allude to another world, one which is more profoundly ours."

Juan López Moctezuma

"How did you get into moviemaking, after being a jazz specialist, and having worked so much in radio?"

"Well, to begin with—I always wanted to make movies. My first childhood memory is about when I was able to go alone to the theater across from my house. It was the old Primavera Theater, and I lived directly across the street from it. From the time I was five years old, they let me go alone. Entering that world was for me the discovery of a vocation. Every day I went to the movies—every day. There were films that I saw as many times as they ran them."

"What kind of films did the Primavera run? I remember a streetcar line that had this name. Did it go by there?"

"Exactly."

"Seems to me—along Baja California?"

"Yes. The streetcar came and went along the sides of the theater. The films were always accompanied by the clickety-clack of the streetcars. But the films were always double or triple features, and they were the great films. Those double features always had the classic horror movies, the classic adventure movies. My first big purchase—representing an outlay of some twenty or twenty-five pesos—was a hand-run projector. It was the simplest kind made: it had a metal box, a lens, and a crank. Along with the projector, and included in the price of twenty-five pesos, I got a cowboy picture, which was two minutes and forty-three seconds long. That cowboy picture is undoubtedly the most-shown film in the history of movies. I played it forward, backward, in slow motion. Since the projector was run by hand, I could adjust the speed according to my needs: I used to run it at high speeds, then rewind it, load it, and reload it. It was then, when I got that machine, that I perceived very clearly the magic of movies. In our century, this magic has been captured. It's caught in technique. Movies, even in their most rudimentary, most commercial form, are inherently magic. If we think about the fact that the most insignificant piece of celluloid is taking a moment in time, freezing it, capturing it—that it enables everyone to relive this moment every time this piece of celluloid is run through the projector—then we clearly understand that magic effectively exists. Pedro Infante films are still shown—very successfully—on Mexican television. Pedro Infante continues to be alive. The cinema lets us see him breathe, walk, enjoy life, sing . . ."

"Isn't it true that many people think he is not dead?"

"Of course. Movies have given Pedro a sort of immortality. If this isn't magic, I don't know what is. For spectators, seeing Pedro Infante or Marilyn Monroe on the screen is the same as watching a real person. Don't you think so? If before our eyes, our minds, our senses, the cinematographic illusion is so effective, we can only acknowledge it: magic is with us, thanks to the technology of the twentieth century. Videotape, film's brother, is also a magical phenomenon par excellence. This tape recorder you're using," continues López Moctezuma with growing enthusiasm, "is a magical artifact. It is grasping a moment in time, in this case a moment of sound.

"Right now I'm working on a story that will express this idea. It goes more or less like this. A film director loses his wife. She dies—and he decides to reconstruct her. First he turns to traditional magic; then to technology. Technical reconstruction allows him to recover her—in reality—with all the senses but one, touch. Through film he reconstructs her and fills his house, a white house, with projections of her physical presence. By magnetic recordings which he had made of her during her lifetime, he has her, for example, answer the telephone, and walk through the house. But the final sense, the one he cannot recapture, is touch. We still don't have the magic with which to preserve tactile sensations—even though we have it to catch time, freeze it, and reproduce it as often as we like. For these reasons, moviemaking attracted me. I was always an imaginative child, a very neurotic one, almost schizophrenic. That is, I was sort of crazy in the strict sense of the word. I was a tortured child. Then, on finding an element . . ."

"Were you an only child?"

"No, I have a younger brother. There were three of us, but the youngest one died . . . on my saint's day actually. My father died when I was six, and my mother began to work as a nurse to support us. My father was a very important criminal lawyer. And he was a judge. He dealt with cases like that of Romero Carrasco. Besides that, he was a writer and a cartoonist of renown. He published various books, wrote for *El Universal,* and did murals for the Free Law School, of which he was a graduate. My father thought I should follow his legal footsteps. They always had the idea that I would be a great lawyer like my father. They always pushed me along that road, and I, with the active imagination that I had . . ."

"Did you read much?"

"Yes, I read a lot. I have some relatives, cousins, who had tons of books. Every Saturday I went to visit them. They were so nice: they not only gave me clothes, they gave me books. I always left their house loaded with all kinds of books. Things like *The Adventures of Tarzan, Pinocho, Chapete,* and the entire *Salgari* series. All, of course, were imaginative works. Wildly so. From there I moved on to important literature—you can put important in quotes—and (although I'm getting away from the theme a little bit), I'd always say that I'm a defender of the lesser arts. I specialized in jazz, which is, of course, considered minor music, and in some cases despised. I'm the most important comicologist in Latin America. That's going to bother Alejandro Jodorowski and Carlos Monsiváis a lot."

"Did you buy a lot of comics?"

"Oh yes. I always did. I bought all the comics. Of course there were three or four and they cost ten centavos ... Chamaco, Pepín, Paquito. Besides that, I went downtown every day to buy North American comics. That's how I learned to speak English. I don't know that speaking English is necessarily a positive attribute."—López Moctezuma returns to the thread of previous conversation. "Still, I was geared to a career in law. Then I wasn't opposed to the idea because law as my father dealt with it was extraordinarily attractive. There were still juries, and the lawyer using surprise tactics could get an acquittal or a guilty verdict. That gave rise to an illusion which was later reinforced when I read the Perry Mason books. Perry was an actor par excellence. He used to place himself center stage, and with theatrical tricks he always won, right? For a long time I thought, mistakenly of course, that that's how law was in Mexico. That that was how our lawyers worked. And it was that misconception that led me to the Free Law School. I began legal studies, and also began to work as a legal assistant for a company called Basham and Ringe. It was one of those very, very large companies. And I realized, with horror and loathing that, among us, the profession was reduced to presenting and receiving writs: replying; waiting for copies; and so on ad infinitum.

"It really grieved me," he continued, "to live in the most sad, sordid, and least imaginative world possible. I decided to get out of law, and I did it surgically. Besides, I was a bad student, and a bad assistant. My only real obligation was to review the Law Bulletin daily, the thing which the Tribunals put out, to see which of our cases had been resolved and how. Get this, in spite of the simpleness of it, I didn't even do that. I didn't have the least vocation. The critical moment had to come, and I grabbed it. It involved an exam which I failed. The professor told me: 'Look, you did very badly, but since I knew your father, and he was such an excellent lawyer, I'm going to pass you.' I told him, no, please ... begged him, because of the memory of my father, to have the good grace to fail me. And I added very seriously that in this moment I was getting out of law because it did not interest me in the least."

Now some years later, López Moctezuma reproduces a sigh

A scene from *La mansión de la locura,* based on a story by Edgar Allan Poe

of relief which must then have represented both an uprooting and an act of liberation.

"From there I jumped into painting, the theater, and began a long series of adventures which landed me in Tijuana where I sold souvenirs and began my career as a radio announcer," he continued. "I spent several months in the North, then returned to the capital, where my family was still hoping I'd resume my legal studies. I took part in two theatrical works. And an uncle of mine, with every good intention, had me put away in a ranch so that I could not play a part that had been given to me. All in all, I went through much resistance and anxiety until there was no doubt that I would not be a lawyer. And that I would dedicate myself to the world of show business.

"It was a lovely time," López Moctezuma reflects, with a tone of voice that indicates that it really was. "I got into television and had a lot of work. In a single week, imagine this, we would produce up to three works: works as important as *Testigo de cargo*, *Prueba de fuego*, and *Marty*. As is natural, I gained broad experience, which would later be very useful in making movies."

"Did you direct any films then?"

"It wasn't possible. Then it was a very hard thing to do, although I think the field is even more closed now to new directors. Before, an aspiring director had only to have directed a film five weeks. That was not so very little since five weeks implied a lot of money. And it was not easy to understand how a producer was going to trust large interests to a novice. But, in short, the situation now is worse. In the case of the section that Rogelio* directs, the doors are firmly closed."

"How then did you continue your career?"

"I acted as director's assistant to Seki Sano. I took part, for example, in the set design of *La Mandrágora*. Then, using my own money, I made a film called *Dios y libertad* or *Tierra de sombras*. With that I won one of the Bellas Artes contests."

Only Satisfaction without Material Benefits

"And after that, it was smooth sailing for you?"

"Hardly. The prize gave me a great deal of satisfaction, but nothing else. That's what tends to happen with those things."

"Even in the case of those you won for *La mansión de la locura?*"

"Those gave me a good deal more satisfaction. They indicate that my film is good enough to compete internationally. But that's all. Don't think that thanks to prizes I can get more work. The same thing always happens to me. Just like with the prizes I won for my work as an announcer. From them I did not get a single other commercial. I even think, coming back to *La*

*Rogelio González; see page 21 [*Trans. note*]

mansión de la locura, that prizes have brought me more antipathy than renown. In Mexico, the media are made up of cannibals, you know? Nobody is forgiven a triumph. One director is furious with another for his success, and happy with his failure. The same is true of other fields. Like, for example, painting. Here, in my country, there have been newspapers which persist in minimizing the honors my film won at Avellino. They say it's not the same festival as Cannes. Of course it's not. But it is an important festival. It's as if to set a standard, I invented Italy, doesn't it seem that way to you? *La mansión* was given prizes in a festival that has been going on for fourteen years, and in which judges include such famous cineasts as Cesare Zavatini and Vittorio de Sica."

"Then the festivals don't really do very much?"

"Well, of course they do. In the first place, as I told you, to win is always satisfying; and more so when competing against the best in the world. In the second place, the prize opens doors for your film. It has an effect on the box office, which in turn has other repercussions, all of them favorable. There is automatic and very effective publicity. In spite of the fact that there are so many advantages," López Moctezuma is quiet for a minute, "I do not think I'll participate in any more festivals."

"Do adverse reactions bother you that much?"

"No. If I abstain, it won't be for that. It will be because of something else. How can I describe it to you? I want to be an artist, and I value what I do highly. It doesn't seem quite right to me to take part in a contest, as if my films were pedigreed dogs, so that a group of men can examine and judge them. I don't know. I just do not like it. I can't complain, mind you. Here in Mexico *La mansión* has been nominated for many prizes. It won over a film by De Anda called *Indio* which ought to be pretty good, since critics and people in general speak wonders of it. But things have not gone badly for me. On the contrary . . ."

"So you do not consider prizes to be a necessary part of a filmmaker's vita?"

"No way. Chaplin never got any. Now they've given him an Oscar, but for his work in general and, I think, because of his age."

"In a word, you're satisfied with the honors conferred on you, but not happy."

"Or happy, but not satisfied. Whichever you wish."

How a Film Director Gets Started

I'm probably wasting the interview, I think to myself as I listen to López Moctezuma. At the beginning of the conversation he discussed a number of very fascinating things. López Moctezuma became enthusiastic remembering Salgari and his Malaysian tigers; and he also told me—at the exact moment when I was changing the cassette in the tape recorder—of what happened to him in Count Dracula's castle, of his love for ghost stories. López Moctezuma is an encyclopedia in which childhood memories flow together—with illustrations by Billiken, rhythms from New Orleans, pieces of Mamerto and Flash Gordon . . . But he's speaking of movies.

"How did you finally decide to go into moviemaking?"

"Let me tell you. I started a company, along with another man, which was going to produce film shorts. Just the two of us it was. He put up the money, and I put up the work. The truth is that I really worked. I did everything: photographing, reading the scripts after having written them, dubbing in the voices of the actors, editing—in short, everything. The deal was that when the business got bigger, I'd get half. The business grew, but my associate explained to me that I had misunderstood: that I could keep working for him but without remuneration other than my salary. I got angry, I got bitter, and, naturally, I quit. But the bitterness didn't last long. I understood that, in the end, I had acquired valuable experience. I had learned everything—or almost everything—that a filmmaker should know. And this knowledge was worth more than the money.

"So, all in all," continues López Moctezuma, "things were not easy. Where was I going to find a producer who would want to risk his money on someone without any background? In order to break into movies, I had to collaborate in the founding of another company, the one that produced *Fando y Lis.*"

"How did that company come about?"

A Work Not Appreciated

"Well, you see, I had directed some plays in the Casa de la Paz. Alejandro Jodorowski also worked there. We used to alternate. He would direct one work, then I would do another. One fine day I took him home with me and we had a long talk. We agreed that our work was not appreciated. We were right. Look, Alejandro, Gurrola and other directors have made montages superior to those you can see in Paris or New York. I'm not exaggerating. Nonetheless, neither in Casa del Lago nor in Casa de la Paz is there even a slightly big public—twenty persons, thirty. At the most, fifty. Alejandro and I reflected on this and thought about it. The best solution was to look for the moviegoing public. Alejandro had a student whose father was rich. That's how we got the funding to make *Fando y Lis.* The film was made at a killing pace. We worked Saturdays and Sundays, and a few weekdays—but the latter always at the cost of leaving aside paid work. You will remember that this film was the cause of a big scandal. It even contributed to to the suspension of a film festival. The lid was put on it for about four years because permission to show it could not be obtained. That was logical because in Acapulco, during the film festival, the army had to intervene to protect us."

The Pressures of the Old Mexican Film Industry

"What caused the reactions? The public?"

"No, not the public. I have always believed that pressures by the old Mexican film industry were at the bottom of it. To be more exact, it made the pressure. But perhaps I'm using the terms unjustly. This 'old Mexican film industry' is very imprecise. The Mexican film industry of the era of *Fando y Lis*—an industry on the decline—caused the pressure. We should not get confused. Our film industry had a golden age during which authentic figures like El Indio Fernández, Ismael Rodríguez, and Fernando de Fuentes excelled. Talented and honest workers. That was followed, however, by the age of the hucksters. They made purposely bad films, based on the deplorable supposition that the public could not understand anything else. Small wonder, then, that this class of moviemakers—if you can call it a class—considered *Fando y Lis* a subversive film. The reaction against it was based on the instinct for self-preservation. They felt that somehow this would work against them. It was simply a matter of honest versus bungled movies. That's why they kept *Fando y Lis* under wraps during these four years I told you about. Outside the country, however, the film caused great interest and got good critiques. It did not earn any money, but it did make possible the filming of *El topo*, which has been a great artistic success and has brought millions of pesos into the box offices."

"How did you manage the foreign distribution?"

"By dint of sacrifices. It is very hard to break into media which have been closed for a long time. Only with quality can it be done. And this is the only road to salvation for the Mexican film industry."

Our Weak Natural Market

"I say that this is the only road because we cannot avail ourselves of the *natural market.* It comprises a large percentage of illiterates. I say this without the least disdain for this public. Disdain would be unjust. They are not responsible for the state of submission in which they have been kept for many years by the bad governments of many countries to the south. Illiteracy and lack of cultural education are facts. The worst thing is that our "huckster" filmmakers—when they thought about it—conducted themselves in the easiest and most negative way. They believed that these depressing circumstances constituted an advantage, and lowered the level of their films.

What they accomplished was to place the Mexican cinema in its current situation—one of division. The punishment fits the crime. And it's obvious that what is going on now is a raising of the quality of production. We have the whole world before us, but we will not gain a place in it except with good films."

"Well, what a miserable criterion existed at that time!"

"Miserable and unworthy. The rationale of 'we're going to give them a low-level product since it satisfies them' only reveals narrowness of spirit and lack of ambition. It has led to pessimism and sparseness. We have them satisfied with a lowly taco instead of trying for a good pastry. At the bottom of it all is the inferiority complex which, not for nothing, has been attributed to us. Not only cineasts, but also critics, have brought this on. 'We don't have the ingredients, we don't have the tradition, we don't have anyting,' they've diagnosed."

"And what can be done to shed this attitude?"

"First, put aside that complex. We should become ambitious people. I think I see in our era a sort of prostration of things Mexican. The generations of some years past had more push. There is no other way of explaining Diego Rivera, Orozco, Siqueiros, Vasconcelos, or Alfonso Reyes. All of them took part in a stellar moment of our culture. They did not stop to figure out their strength, they acted, they created a work, and that work was on a par with that of writers and painters of any other country. Currently, Cuevas and Fuentes—both of whom I personally admire very much—have reached only a few other countries. They haven't won the prestige that the other artists had."

"And to what is this due?"

"It is possible that there are political reasons. During the Cárdenas* era, there were still very real evidences of revolutionary fervor. Mexicans were proud of our country. We were conscious of the fact that we had made a very inspiring social movement; that in many senses we were making history. This was reflected in art. It prompted a nationalism, but a nationalism, understand, neither modest nor mediocre, but enthusiastic and at the same time sensible; one disposed to capture the admiration and respect of other countries."

*Lázaro Cárdenas, president (1934–40) [*Trans. note*]

Another scene from *La mansión de la locura*

The Mexican Nationalistic Cinema

"As is natural," contines López Moctezuma, "the cinema also captured these attitudes. El Indio Fernández dealt with them, the same as Ismael Rodríguez. And speaking of Ismael Rodríguez, I think that he is one of our most gifted cineasts. Currently he's suffering the contempt of our critics because he does not share their ideology. It is a criticism which has not yet learned to use strictly cinematic criteria."

"What does guide Mexican criticism?"

"Usually ideology—or even pettier and more irrelevant facts: for example, whether or not you belong to one or another clique."

"And are its opinions reflected at the box office?"

"Fortunately, no. The criticism is so obviously partisan that nobody pays any attention to it. How can you take Ayala Blanco seriously—for example—if he takes advantage of every film to make bad jokes? He is not interested in the films. The only thing that matters to him is showing off his genius."

"It is pure baroqueness besides . . ."

"Baroqueness and humor, putting the latter word in quotes. The cinema is a cover for him: it allows him to show off his talent, also in quotes, and demonstrate his humor, naturally in quotes. He also uses his ideology, which as such I respect, but the way he uses it . . . For him important films are those that have cost blood, sweat, and tears—likewise in quotes. For example, if a young man with a Super-8 camera goes out one morning to make a movie, this young man is a hero of the art, and his film is sensational. That is, for Ayala Blanco the quality of the films depends on the simplicity of the means used to make them. If I have seventy-five pesos and a defective camera, and I spend eight hours of my time photographing these bricklayers working in the building next door, then I'm worthy of high praise. He would call me a revolutionary because I committed the heroic feat of filming outside the establishment, and because I eluded union, political, and social rules. Leaving aside considerations about the intrinsic quality of the product—which are the most important ones—it is obvious that you cannot compare this elementary filmmaker with another who puts forth tremendous efforts to get ahold of two million pesos—which is easier said than done—and puts himself up against a very solid structure. This does not even account for the fact that he is responsible to twenty or forty people who work with him for the success of that work, as well as for the economic gains and prestige which they may win or lose with him."

"What is the greatest duty of a film director?"

The Duty of the Director: Honesty

López Moctezuma answers without hesitation:

"To be honest. This answer means more than meets the eye. To be honest means taking the cinema seriously, putting the five senses and all the intellectual and moral powers into the good execution of the work. The dishonest director is the one who makes bad films, knowing what he is doing. It is the commercial director, who does not see the cinema as art but only as industry, and who very carefully works to make money. To him the public and his personal honor matter not at all. A cinematic official has expressed the idea that cinema is an industry and nothing more. This opinion is lamentable. In it all the mishaps which have befallen us are pronounced. If we don't agree on the artistic angle; if we don't believe that the cinema, as an art, has to be concerned with raising the spiritual and cultural levels of the spectators; if we insist that the spectators are a bunch of idiots and that it is not worth the trouble to give them high-quality products since they're not going to understand them, if we do all these things, then we condemn our cinema forever.

"The bad thing is that the cinema is an activity from which a good many people earn a living, which could give the country a good deal of prestige, and which has a respectable tradition. All this does not mean," he continued, "that one has to ignore the industrial side of cinema. Of course, moviemaking is an industry and involves large investments. For this reason it requires a respectable income which will bring it profits. But these truths are not contradictory. Instead they're complementary. In order for a film to be a box-office attraction, it must be good. Anything else is sophistry, a fallacy. Bad films or box-office attractions are only relative and temporary. You have, on the other hand, the case of *Cabaret*, which has filled our theaters for months. It is a work full of cinematic value, even though the critics persist in demolishing it. It is possible that from the point of view of ideas, the film may not be very praiseworthy. I'm speaking of cinematography, and *Cabaret* is very well made. It has quality which it would be stupid to deny."

"Aren't there signs that this way of thinking is changing?"

"So it seems, fortunately. I believe that in Mexico honest people are beginning to reappear. I think that each day we can count on a greater number of cineasts who wish to make good movies, and who aren't going along with any type of fakery, like selling a mule for a horse, and saying that the public is ignorant and doesn't deserve anything more because it would not understand it. There are many of these new people. Some may be mistaken: others are not. Some probably have talent even though others lack it. That is not what matters. What ought to encourage us is that all these directors and actors, writers and others, are truly practicing their vocation."

"To what do you attribute our present low rate of production?"

"It is the result of total irresponsibility at all levels. Look, Mexico could be one of the cinematic capitals of the world. It has all the requisites. For example, it has natural conditions like its climate. Here in our country we have two months of rain per year, and the other ten months are perfect for outdoor filming. We have the added advantage that our landscapes are beautiful. I never tire of quoting Malcolm Lowry, the author of *Under the Volcano,* who said—more or less: 'In Mexico, one finds himself in a Greek landscape, but two kilometers distant there is a desert, and three kilometers distant, a jungle.' And, in effect, our land is so rich in settings that it's like one giant movie set. The desert in *Fando y Lis* is near here, in Texcoco; other country scenes from the same movie are found two blocks from this building in the suburb of del Valle. In order to film *La mansión de la locura,* I only had to go a half a kilometer from here . . .

"Also," continues López Moctezuma, "our technicians excel in their capability. There would be no serious obstacle, then, to making excellent films."

"And why aren't they made?"

"We're confronted with an administrative behavior so deficient . . . and then there are absurd problems like those which are due to the union question."

"There are two unions in the industry. Is this the reason for the problems?"

"From our point of view, it determines them. As you know, there is, on the one hand, the Cinematographic Production Workers Union, whose directors are headed by one Rogelio González, a good-for-nothing director. He obstructs the entrance of any living being into the union, and in this way curbs one of the fundamental rights of Mexican citizens: the right to work and the expression of ideas. For example, according to him, I am not a film director."

"How have you new directors been able to direct? Because the fact is that you have directed films."

"Illegally. There are twenty-two of us directors in the same situation: making our films clandestinely. This is the way, for example, that Paul Leduc worked to produce *Reed, México Insurgente;* Corkidi to make *Ángeles y querubines;* and Gómez to make *La fórmula secreta.* To disguise them, these were all filmed as shorts. *La mansión de la locura* was filmed in three parts: three shorts that were put together. The other union, STIC,* doesn't make absurd demands. It has no great desire to keep us out, but among its sections there is none that covers directors of long films. Thus, we belong to that union, but we have to resort to this gambit."

"And why aren't there loud and organized protests?"

"Perhaps because of fear. I know of cases in which the fear is evident. In my case, whenever I can, I complain and protest in public. Of course the reactions haven't given much hope."

"All right, but there hasn't always been this turmoil. In fact, the film competition for new directors seems to indicate a calming down."

"I agree. That was an easier time. But even then, the young generation wasn't received very willingly. Gurrola had great success with his *Tajimara,* but hasn't done anything else that hasn't been 16 or 8 millimeters. Also *Tajimara* was not shown commercially until several years later, and then it was under another name: *Los bienamados.*"

"You're right. And up to now the competition has not been repeated."

"No. And Rogelio González has become even more dictatorial. A little while ago some of his comments were published in the newspaper. They were monstrous. He said that in view of the national film crisis, no new directors would be admitted to the union, nor would he consent to a repetition of the case of *Reed, México Insurgente* and *Los meses y los días* which have been shown commercially. As I said, this is monstrous, and even more so if you consider the fact that the two films had considerable success with the public."

*Sindicato de Trabajadores de la Industria Cinematográfica [*Trans. note*]

"How did you manage to get *La mansión de la locura* shown?"

"That's another story. It's because it won international prizes, like *Reed, México Insurgente* and *Ángeles y querubines.* Echeverría, who, I have to admit, has done a lot to help our film industry and who is seriously trying to solve its problems, has made the winning films examples. This is why there weren't major problems in showing them. Even so, *La mansión* had to wait two years to be shown. Of course, that's better than the four years that *Fando y Lis* had to wait."

"It still seems strange to me that you became a film director. I return to my first question: how did you jump from radio and other things, from jazz and the theater, to film directing?"

"I told you. Movies are for me a magical instrument. Magic unto themselves. It's a way of building other worlds. I admire Meliés, who was capable of suspecting this and using all these possibilities. Moviemaking has another aspect, also important. That is the reporting aspect. I also admire Lumière, who was the first to see and take advantage of that. But I prefer Meliés and his infinitely mysterious and promising pictures. For reasons of temperament this is the kind of movie I accept as mine. It's a kind of alchemy, science, occult art."

"The Mexican film industry is tied to reality, don't you think?"

"Yes, but at the same time, it's very remote, very far from reality. Cardboard people are presented as real people. Thus you have excellent actors like Arturo de Córdoba, who were wasted. Arturo de Córdoba didn't exist because his characters never existed. For their true realism, I have the utmost respect for Ismael Rodríguez and the Buñuel of *Los olvidados.* In order to be realists, they did not make up a fictitious reality; rather they used true reality."

"This lack of imagination is strange when in Mexico we're so given to fables."

"Of course. Mexico is a surrealistic country. Breton discovered that. And in Mexico the works of Remedios Varo and Leonora Carrington have been presented. In short, it's a mystery. Why do we persist in being realistic, but misrepresent reality, ending up with a false realism which is deformed, but not recognized as being deformed? Who knows why.

"The thing is that our film industry, with all of its problems and contradictions, counts on you and on the tremendous vitality of the new generation, as well as of the older one. I have faith in this industry and I think that you do too. If not, you wouldn't be involved in it. The very presence of a person like Rodolfo Echeverría seems to open up new horizons. It seems that you yourself, as unconventional as you are, suspected this just a short while ago."

"Yes, but Echeverría is a person, and like all people, will someday disappear from the industry. Then what's going to happen? We need institutions, or better said, we need to clean up the institutions. And that . . ."

The phrase is left hanging. I leave López Moctezuma with his Poe-like shadows, his Bosch-like imaginings, with his likes and dislikes.

9

 Jorge Fons

Jorge Fons is in his office in the suburb of Nápoles. It is a pretty office, with modern, comfortable furnishings, with a view of much of the city. This is where the film-producing company, of which Fons is one of the principal heads, works. When I arrive, Fons, very busy typing, is sitting between cushions and glass partitions. The director of *Los cachorros* explains that at the moment he is working on two things. It doesn't seem like much to him, but in reality it must be a lot of work. I first speak to him of that last film which has just prompted both eulogies and insults, and which has been showing, at the theater where it premiered, many more weeks than some critics predicted.

"There are those who will challenge the film's lack of fidelity to Vargas Llosa's story," I say to Fons.

"Well, look, it's a relative lack of fidelity. I believe that the literary work, like the artistic or dramatic, has the ability to awaken a whole series of ideas, and that to expound these ideas doesn't mean betraying the work. The finished work is a point of arrival because in it all the efforts of the creator culminate. But it is also a point of departure. From this work many stimuli and questions occur to those who know the work. The same thing happens with any other object of our experience. If any scene whatsoever from real life is produced in front of us, we have the right to use it for our own ends."

"But isn't there a kind of lack of respect when someone takes a literary product and models it arbitrarily?"

"I don't think so. I insist that art is not used up in one statement. I even told Vargas Llosa some time ago that *Los cachorros* could lend itself to an indefinite number of films. Of all the roads that book opened, I chose one. There is a first choice which is the one that directs us to one specific story, and not to another. After that first choice we also select a means of treating the story, the point of view which best accommodates our feeling and what we want to express."

"Are you happy with that film?"

"I don't believe so. Too many things have happened because of it: not just since it's been shown, but since the project first began."

"Can you tell me about them?"

"Well . . . it's such a bitter experience, and so many people have talked about it, that I'd like to be the exception and remain silent. I prefer to consider it a step, one more step that brings me closer to the kind of cinema I really want to make. If I have to be honest, *El Quelite* is much more interesting to me. It involves an idea that I didn't like, but one that eventually captivated me. It is from a very silly satire, and for me was a very important experience. It made me work with resources other than my own."

"Did you direct *Jory?*"

"Yes. That was another accidental thing. I definitely am inclined to believe that the cineast has to be receptive to all these accidental things. And the truth is that it shouldn't have to be that way, but things have a way of occurring when you least expect them to."

"Before you made movies, what did you do?"

"Well, there's almost no 'before.' That is, all my life I've worked in film. I studied it very early on. I have done some theater, but overall, cinematography has interested me. In

A scene from *Fé, esperanza y caridad* with Katy Jurado

CUEC,* in books, in New York . . . I've been a cameraman, an editor, I've made publicity shorts, and acted as an assistant director."

The Cineast Should Be Committed to Himself

"Do you think that the cineast should be committed?"

"Yes, to himself. This is the greatest and truest commitment. I can't commit myself to you if I haven't previously committed myself to me."

*Centro Universitario de Estudios Cinematográficos (University Center of Cinematographic Studies) [*Trans. note*]

"But shouldn't the cineast have a commitment to the society in which he lives?"

"I insist that there is no greater commitment than that made to oneself. You could tell me that filmmaking, because of its power to reach the public represents a huge responsibility. You could argue that I, a film director, have more serious obligations than the elevator operator in this building."

I'm on the verge of telling Fons that the building's elevator is automatic, but I keep quiet. It would be an impertinent reply.

"You could tell me all this," he continues, "but I will always believe that, basically, the problem of all human life revolves around mankind, and that no one is closer to anyone than we each are to ourselves."

"That is your point of departure . . . All right, but in reality it seems obvious to me that in each of your works there is a little—or a lot—of the man named Jorge Fons."

"Of course. But not in the sense that the work has an autobiographical bent. What happens, and we get back to the same thing, is that each work has some relativity to man, and no man is closer to the work than the author."

Good Cinema Is Always Revolutionary

"What kind of man interests you? Man in general?"

"Men like us."

"And for our Mexican way of being what kind of cinema would be most appropriate? Do you believe that young filmmakers here in Mexico are on the right track? Because there are cineasts from previous generations who say that the new ones haven't contributed anything; that the only thing that distinguishes them is their audacity."

"I don't think any determined form, from the cinematic point of view, corresponds to any particular people or region. Ethnicity, or economic and political circumstances, don't have a direct or necessary relation to art. I think a well-done film is one favorable to man, solely because it is well done. Theme and other factors are not important. In the end, they're circumstantial."

"Is the leftist film industry, the revolutionary film industry, then unimportant?"

"It seems to me that revolutionary films are what all of us should be doing, but I don't mean to equate 'revolutionary' with 'leftist.' That is, there is no direct relationship between one concept and the other. Quality cinema is revolutionary cinema, and it is quality cinema that has something to offer man."

I hazard an interpretation of these ideas. "For example, *The Damned* . . . ?"

"Well, yes. Undoubtedly it is great cinema. We can pigeon-hole that film according to its theme, its style, its period. But beyond that, there is something else. The great quality of Visconti is above and beyond that. And his work demonstrates revolutionary character because it speaks to us of man, of his mortal and divine possibilities."

"According to these criteria, what do you think of El Indio Fernández?"

"I respect El Indio very much, because he's a good cineast, and because in some way he has achieved magnificent moments in his films. That he puts our country's peasants on the screen, that he uses the figure of the charro, has nothing to do with the value of his work. It can be right on the mark, or lamentable, but that doesn't matter to us. What matters is the quality, which is often confused with the ability to stir up human beings to their very depths."

The Search for Lost Time

"Don't you believe," I ask Fons, "that the Mexican film industry has been deceiving the public? It presents a world that doesn't exist, and places its characters in unreal situations."

"What I believe, apart from the problems of the Mexican film industry or any other country's film industry, is that this artistic product, simply by its aspirations to be that, has to realize certain functions. To put it more clearly, it has to aspire to certain objectives. If these objectives aren't determined, its artistry will be invalidated. The thing is, all the moments that make up our life are significant, and of consequence, although

A scene from *Los cachorros*

we may not realize that at first glance. We each live such and such an amount of time, and this time goes on filling up with moments—in appearance, simple moments. But all you have to do is scratch the surface of these moments and you find their substance. What matters to us? We know that we have to eat, sleep, work, fulfill certain physical, sexual, and intellectual necessities throughout this amount of time that we're in the world. We also know that we have to surround ourselves with people who afford us friendship, and with others to whom we can give love, hate, or knowledge. And all this is for what? I think it's for something, although this something often escapes us. There are times when we manage to grasp it, and some of us even bring to life an ambition of higher order which is to mold ourselves. Consider the importance of that: to mold, not pieces of knowledge, because in the end they don't tell us anything, but the significance of these pieces of knowledge. To go beyond a simple story, to put yourself into it. Chalo Laiter told me once, and I agree with him, that it's necessary to give a product a determined density. I understand what he means: he is not talking about grammatical density; he's talking about something else."

"Then, for you, this is making films."

"Making films, or life, or whatever. In the work is where you learn something truly substantial. One can learn to know oneself."

Cinema and the Third World

Jorge Fons puts things in such a way that they do not have much to do with pure anecdote. He wants cinema and believes that once it's obtained, everything else will follow. I think I understand his ideas but, although it seems pointless I insist: "Isn't there any way that we can get rid of the conventionalisms, the cardboard scenes, the actors who move like puppets, in the Mexican cinema?"

"In all this, there are good intentions. But for my part, I'm convinced that good cinema isn't going to be achieved by decrees or force, or good will. I insist that good cinema comes from more profound impulses. I think, for example, of the needs of Latin American countries. From what we've just discussed you can guess what I'm going to say: that Latin American cinema has no obligation to indicate these needs to be good, to be leftist, to be revolutionary, or even Third World. I can understand the deprivations that our countries suffer. I can clearly identify the enemies, and can realize the problems facing them—problems of subjugation, exploitation, colonialism. We can look at the cinema as a useful weapon, as an instrument capable of freeing us from these constraints, or at least of helping us fight them. I can totally agree with this kind of thinking. I even believe that, along with television and other media that disseminate ideas, the cinema could place itself at the service of our cause. It could help in the fight against underdevelopment. It could contribute to straightening out our history, which has cost us so much . . ."

Fons leaves the words hanging in the air, as though to leave me hanging on them, waiting for what will follow.

"But," he continues in full voice, "then we wouldn't be talking about cinema. I'm part of the independent cinema, of the Third World cinema. I'm unconditionally part of the Super-8 group, which I see as a great stronghold. But I'm not part of all of them because they're going to bring on the revolution. They're going to help make films, and by those the revolution, but first things first."

"What is the Super-8 group?"

"Well, Super-8 is a means of making films. It is very economical and simple; so much so that a fifteen-year-old kid could do it. Imagine what happens when a youth sees the possibility of shouting with a camera about what he wants. It gives him a freedom that no other cinema offers. To him, the cinema is a personal affair—without the problems of cost, censorship, or industrialization. Around this system, a group of people like Héctor Abadié and Sergio García has formed. They're doing good work and achieving levels of cinema that are very appealing."

"To pin it down, what is the cinema?"

"The possibility of creating in images the significant things of life. It's not really very complicated. Sometimes we confuse ourselves because we begin by talking about the cinema, and end up arguing about the film industry, or social and economic problems of Mexico, Latin America, or the Third World."

What Cinema Lacks: A Love of the Work

"Well and good, Mr. Fons, but there are times when you don't distinguish between cinema and the film industry. It could be that what one says about the first also fits the second. For example, what is our cinema's greatest sin? The reply could be that it embraces both films and the industry."

"I believe that the greatest sin of our cinema is a lack of love. Let me explain: whoever undertakes a job ought to put some passion into it. A passion that makes him do the best possible work. This applies to any activity we can think of. I believe that, as long as one isn't a moral idiot, if you start a nail factory, the nails have to be made with love, in the sense I spoke of. It would be stupid to make bad ones, not because the business would ultimately fold, but because there would be a sort of self-betrayal in each piece deliberately or negligently defective. I'm not sure I'm explaining myself but it's very clear to me. If a producer didn't want his film to be good in the first place, he would be ridiculous. He could earn money, accumulate a fortune, but he wouldn't have fulfilled his principal objective, that of putting authentic films on the market."

"What do you think of Fernando de Fuentes?"

"I think he is a unique and admirable figure in our film industry. You see, he was a director and also a producer; and he left an *oeuvre* full of integrity. He also managed to make a revolutionary cinema, not because it has cowboys and people with chinstraps on horseback, but pure and simple, because of its high quality. I have great affection for De Fuentes. And just think, he's gone but he stays among us because his films endure. Isn't this what we all basically ought to pursue?"

I leave the question hanging and say good-bye to Fons, who looks at me very seriously and smiles under his enormous mustache.

10

José Estrada

José Estrada is another representative of Mexico's new cinema. I've interviewed him in bits and pieces: first in the lobby of the theater where *El profeta Mimí* premiered, in a special showing for the press; afterward in a Yucatecan restaurant across the street; and later at the La Tecla in the Pink Zone. He has the air of a sportsman, and in fact during one of our talks he told me that there was a time when he dedicated himself to soccer. Now cinema is the dominant activity in his life, almost his obsession, after his work in theater, radio, and other similar media.

"You may not believe," he says to me while eating some *burritas* in the long-established restaurant, "that I still have to do things that you would call peripheral but which enable me to survive. A film director works on his own stuff in a rather sporadic manner, as is natural, although his needs remain constant. Before *El profeta Mimí* I worked on a couple of Chabelo's films, and also on a *fotonovela*. Logical, because it's

127

indispensable, even though one would like to spend all his time on what he considers really important."

Salvador, my husband, who is with us, observes that this is, more or less, the strategy that book publishers follow. They publish a good work that sells badly, and to maintain the business they have to print five or six popular titles.

Salvador comments, "These titles don't bring any praise to the publisher, but they enable him to survive and keep publishing from time to time other really worthwhile books."

An interview, as I said, done in pieces, and naturally choppy and fragmentary. In my notebook and on the tape recorder there are some paragraphs, some questions, that give an idea of how this representative of the present restlessness of our film industry thinks.

To Make a Film: Putting Together a Puzzle

"Is it very difficult to make a film?"

It is almost impossible to speak over the noise in the Gabriel Figueroa Theater. Stars and starlets—I see for example, Fabiola Falcón—critics, writers, and officials congregate in little groups and talk without stopping. I've disengaged myself from Josefina Vicens and Lic. Vega Tato in order to ask Estrada my question. It is not a very opportune time, but he answers in-between greetings and saying thank you to those who are congratulating him.

"Well, look, it's like putting a puzzle together. First, a filmable book, the first piece, appears on the desk. With a reading of the book come notes and ideas which seem to improve the imagined construction of the work. Then comes a tearing down. The elements stand alone, disjointed, and one has to suffer great anguish to give them unity. Filming is a game: a game of moving the pieces around, submerging them in chaos and disorder. At the end of the job, through editing, they once again gain coherence. What was no more than a shadow lodged in the imagination of the creator changes into a tangible reality."

The Director As Providence

"The film director," Estrada tells me one afternoon in La Tecla, a cafe on Copenhague Street, "has many responsibilities. In the first place, he is responsible for the life, character, and behavior of between eighty and a hundred and fifty persons. Therefore, his work has to be very secure, and very technical: he ought to respect the demands of his personal inspiration, the same as those of his work timetable.

"The director, as you know, has another responsibility that could almost be called metaphysical." Estrada has gone from the first idea to a second one which catches his attention more. "The person who is directing a film is the only one who knows for sure what is going to happen, both in the day-to-day reality of the people working with him and also in the imaginary reality of the work. The cameraman, the author, and the producer have no exact idea of the immediate future. The director is the only one who controls the film in his mind. In his work there are varied requirements and impulses. There are incessant question-and-answer games which he, with his power over what will happen, has to go along solving, according to the needs of the moment, but also in accord with his original idea. Through all this he must maintain an order and clarity that would stand an ordeal by fire.

The Cineast's Commitment

"Do you believe," I ask Estrada, "that the cinema is a committed art?"

"I think that it bears an unavoidable commitment, that is, to tell the truth. In a given social context, there are always faults and evils which art cannot ignore, particularly an art like cinema which by its very nature is directed at the masses. Another thing is that the cinema has to suggest solutions. I believe that with the decrying of problems, the commitment is fulfilled. Solutions are not the province of the artist, but of politicians, sociologists, and economists. In Mexico we're in a fairly peculiar position since we demand an attack on capitalism, and at the same time we have to deal with an awkward fact: that our cinema is made possible by capitalists and not by directors."

From the University Theater to *El profeta Mimí*

"Let's see. Tell me something about your career. Is it true that you began in university theater?"

"Yes. I had worked in it, and had put on in El Granero a work of Valle-Inclán's that I like very much, *El retablo de la mujer lujuria.* To my mind it went very well. Of course we had a strong cast, with distinguished names from the cinematic world. For example, Isela Vega, Daniela Rossen, and actors as good as Claudio Obregón and Oscar Chávez were in it. Nonetheless I was saddened by it because the effort had been so great, and the result so good, but the public did not attend. Then Mr. Pérez Gavilán and Mr. Wallerstein, from Cinematográfica Marte, which produced *Los ciafanes,* came to see me. They offered to do a film, and the same thing happened that always happens. I vacillated between my disillusionment which resulted from the little interest my theatrical work had awakened and the feeling of responsibility before the world of cinema, about which I knew nothing. In effect, I didn't have the slightest idea of what it was to make a film, but I realized that the opportunity was unique. I decided to gamble, bet on the cinema, and won. This because actually things went very well with my first work, *Siempre hay una primera vez,* which is made up of three stories. It had rather good critical and box-office success. Since then I've stuck with film. I left Radio Universidad where I was also working and opted to make my living totally from the cinema. Until now I've managed to do that, although of course I made some things for Chabelo and Pepito, as I think I told you another time."

"What amount of work is necessary for a director to support himself and not have to take on lesser jobs?"

"From my own experience I think I'd survive with one film a year. One can adjust his personal budget. What happens is

A scene from *El profeta Mimí*

that there are times when you make a film every three to four years. And that nobody could stand."

The Aggressiveness of the New Cinema

El profeta Mimí pinpoints some very real persons and situations of our country. This is clearly done with an accusatory intent. For example, it shows the bad effect of religion, which is limited to the cult of images and superstitions; in the forefront is a self-sacrificing mother, the ruination of her son; and there is a good part in which the characters find little escape from prostitution and crime. I've talked of these things with José Estrada who is entirely aware of what they could cause.

"The public," I say to him "can stand the nudes in *Naná,* but to mess with religious beliefs may irritate them, don't you think?"

"The worst that could happen is that they crucify me, and then I'd be converted into a religion," Estrada answers with that special tone of voice that old students of Salesian high schools use at times like these.

"On the other hand," he continues, "if it's true that I stuck to negative interpretations of Christianity, I also have to laugh at the other church I invented in the film, whose devotees feel that they're watched by the eyes of God and Nixon."

"And the mother figure," I suggest. "It could be that in her you can find all the symptoms of the transformation of the Mexican cinema. You have to imagine the mother in *El profeta Mimí* thirty years ago, played by Sara García and directed by Ismael Rodríguez."

The Young and the Cinema

"What do youths in Mexico do to learn something about cinema?"

"Well, there is an institute at the National University, the University Center of Cinematographic Studies. Unfortunately, it doesn't work as well as we'd like. One reason is its lack of budget, and the other is its overpopulation. The first-year students are numerous, although most drop out in the second year. This doesn't exactly represent stability. From CUEC there have come three or four directors, but that's it. I get the impression that the kids are fairly confused when they get there. They all want to be directors, but nobody wants to be a photographer, writer, critic, or scenarist. Besides, they are all in a hurry. They won't take an apprenticeship which in reality ought to be pretty rigorous."

"Thus, almost all are self-taught."

"Of course. I've told you some of my life history. I got into films with on-the-spot experience, but obviously lacked specialized training."

"Exactly what was your experience?"

"Well, I'd been a soccer player, as I once told you. I'd attempted painting; I'd even worked in a restaurant somewhere on the road to Toluca. But this is beside the point. What matters is that I'd directed twenty-three plays and done more than a hundred on the radio. I first started in the Molière Theatre, which had very little effect. I went quickly to the Casa del Lago and later was with the University Theater. Then I was titular director of the Theater Department and Radio Universidad, the latter along with Juan Ibáñez. I coordinated the activities of the student theater for eight or ten years. As you can see, I had experience when I got into cinema, but not cinema experience."

"Did you find it hard to adjust to the change in atmosphere?"

"No. To tell the truth, I enjoy covering all fronts. As you saw, *El profeta Mimí* took place among prostitutes, which meant I had to familiarize myself with that atmosphere. I would have done the same if it had taken place among politicians."

"You're comparing prostitution with politics!"

Estrada was amused. "No, I'm not comparing them. On the contrary, I'm citing two extremes."

"All right, so we know that in Mexico we don't have very good places for the preparation of new cineasts. But suppose there is a young director who wants to work. What can he expect?"

"Well, he finds himself facing the union, which, like all unions, protects its members. They try to avoid too much com-

Two scenes from Estrada's *Maten al león,* filmed in Puerto Rico

petition, of which there is plenty since there are one hundred and thirty-six of us directors, and about forty films a year are produced. This means it's not an easy problem. I agree with the need to open the doors so that new elements can enter, but it is also necessary to protect the old ones. When I got into the union, I did it along with five or six other new cineasts—like for example, Laiter, Olhovich, and Hermosillo. This was the assembly's decision, but the same group then returned to its isolation. Based on the new film competition of ten years duration, only Juan Ibáñez and Alberto Isaac have gotten in."

"But there are people, like López Moctezuma, who have been fighting a long time without being allowed in."

Estrada makes an affirmative gesture, like someone who understands the problem.

"What difference is there," I go on, "between filming at the América Studios and the Churubusco Studios?"

"At Churubusco you count on a better technical level, and a larger budget. The Cinematographic Production Workers

Union, which operates at these studios, is also the union which specifically handles long films. This is why there are directors, with proven merit, fighting to get in. Besides López Moctezuma, we could mention Corkidi, Tony Sbert, and others."

"What worries me is that there is a group of little old men who no longer are directing, but who are in the union, and who influence its decisions."

"Yes. It is not a simple problem. Basically what is happening is that salaries are very low, and also there aren't any retirement funds. This last is important and someone should take note of it."

"To finish, are there countries where the cineast's professional studies are a little better organized than ours?"

"Of course there are. In the socialist countries there are university programs, just like engineering and medicine. You study for a set number of years, prepare work, do a thesis, and get a degree. Recent graduates are incorporated into the industry as assistants and thus go on learning. At some point they produce shorts, and then later have a shot at long films. It is a very logical sequence. Here in Mexico, in contrast, we are apt to enter a program of absolute improvisation, and do our learning as we go along."

Colophon on Criticism

Once, in La Tecla, I said to Estrada, "All right, we've talked a lot about the cinema. Of the old and new, of the work that the newcomers do to make their initial films. You've even surprised me by saying that even your own experience and lack of knowledge about the atmosphere did not cause you any trauma when you got into the studios."

"And why was I going to suffer a trauma?"

"Well, because of the differences of technique and people. I've always thought that the studio atmosphere is a scandal."

"It is an atmosphere that is neither more nor less turbulent than that of any other activity. Perhaps the difference is that the adulteries and divorces of the stars come out in the newspapers while those of other people are kept secret."

"Can we agree, definitively, that there is a new cinema in Mexico?"

"I believe that our cinema is as new as the needs for expression in the time at hand. These needs are greater than they were twenty years ago. Now one doesn't say on the screen what the public hopes to hear, in line with the old conventionalisms of self-sacrificing mothers, the good poor people, and the bad rich people; or the poor having a lot of fun, and the rich as bored as oysters. All this, it seems to me, is becoming past history. It could be, and from this point of view it would be fitting to speak of a new cinema. But what really has changed is the country's mentality."

"And criticism? How has criticism behaved with relation to you directors?"

"In the 1930s a journalist by the name of Luz Alba was writing; she had very good judgment, knew plenty about cinema, and maintained a congruent line of thought. When she passed from the scene, and Álvaro Custodio left criticism and devoted himself to the theater, criticism was left in the hands of newspaper reporters, and it began to speak of backroom gossip and social events without the least importance. That was when Lumière, Barbien, El Pajarillo Indiscreto, Carl Hillos, and so many others that you and I know appeared. They're not exactly critics because they do short and superficial notices. Any cineast who respects himself needs, from the other side of the desk, more profound critics. Thanks to criticism, it is possible to establish a true dialogue, by which the creator is in a position to correct his faults and perfect his virtues. If criticism goes mute, and deals with frivolity or commercialism, then the dialogue is cut off. Luckily, that sort of void hasn't lasted long. A really key moment was when the magazine *Nuevo Cine* appeared. It was done by a worthwhile and honest group of people, who owed a lot to the sagacity and honesty of Francisco Pina. The film industry needs people like that more now than ever before. While we made films for illiterates, there was no reason for serious columns in the cultural supplements of the newspapers. Now things are different. We can maintain a continuous confrontation with serious opinions."

"So there is serious criticism, apart from newspaper reporting . . ."

"Of course. People like Pérez Turrent, Manuel Michel, García Riera, De la Colina, and Ayala Blanco demand much better cinema than the old one. They make up a group that exerts pressure on us, along with other critics. Like, for example, Carlos Monsiváis, who on Radio Universidad puts forth ferocious and good criticism. There are yet other names, equally good, like La China Mendoza and Nancy Cárdenas. In this way, with the work of this generation of good critics, we're purifying ourselves and the public is refining its taste and judgment."

"Have you been badly treated by the critics?"

"At the subjective level, I could complain because almost none of my films has come through unscathed. I'd like it if they weren't attacked, but obviously that's my problem. On the other hand, I don't have a burning desire to make film expressly for the critics. If that were the case, I'd be adopting an *a priori* position, and that is contrary to all artistic creation."

Sergio Olhovich

It is not necessary to pull words from Sergio Olhovich. One little question is enough to start him developing ideas, slowly, like someone in no hurry. I spoke to him in his small but pleasant office at the Churubusco Studios.

"Is it possible to speak of a change in the mentality of the Mexican cinema?"

"Yes and no. Since more films are being made, naturally more kinds are appearing, and competition is opening up. The other side is that each producer develops his own policy, although I'm afraid they all have the same objective—making money. There aren't any film producers who act as patrons. It would be very good if they existed but I think the government is the only one that fulfills that role."

Cinema, Vocation of the Young

"Why did you dedicate yourself to cinema?"

"From the time I was a boy, I experimented with it. This

wasn't something I was unique in doing: everyone in my generation was. We grew up among the incitements of the cinema. Our culture is, in great part, a cinematic culture."

While Olhovich talks, I try to guess his age. He must be thirty-two or thirty-five years old.

"From the very beginning I found my path. As a first step, I studied theatrical directing with Seki Sano. I started in humanities at UNAM, but didn't finish because I won a scholarship in Russia at the State Institute of Cinema. I spent eight years there in all, six studying and, before that, two learning the language. I traveled a good deal in Russia and had inexhaustible opportunities to meet people, become familiar with other ways of life, et cetera."

"Do you have Russian ancestors?"

"I'm very Mexican, although my surname sounds foreign. When I decided to leave the country, I did it for a very simple reason: it was very hard to break into the film industry which is so closed. CUEC didn't exist; neither did Super-8; or any developed cinema. It was the Industry, period. Industry with the capital 'I,' and impregnable. I tried to get scholarships in various countries, and they gave me one in Russia. I was lucky because they have strong—really very old—cinematographic traditions. In Russia film creators and theorists are working who incessantly look for new styles. The schooling is extremely good, which is a very important advantage to blossoming cineasts, who can study and learn. You get Soviet knowledge of cinema, and along with it that of other countries. And besides that, you have at your disposal extensive materials. Equipment and great technical and economic possibilities. We had the chance to film, and film a lot. This is fundamental because practice is how one becomes a cineast. You encounter real difficulties and perfect your capability."

"But wasn't it hard for you to reconcile your learning in Russia with your character and that of our country?"

"Well, here we're very boxed in by foreign cinema. We have a lot of American and French cinema. Although we also have our own tradition—that of El Indio Fernández, which is the most defined and complete of our nationalism. With these two supports, these two points of view, the Russian experience was but one more advantage for me."

"Then you think that we have a lot of Hollywood influence?"

"Yes. We feel a very strong influence from that cinema from the other side of the border. This isn't bad since United States cinema holds one of the top positions in the world."

The Possibility of a Latin American Cinema

"Do you consider our country's cinema mature?"

"I think we haven't yet reached full potential. Neither have we managed to make a Latin American cinema. To my mind this latter should be one of the goals not only of our filmmakers but also of those in the southern republics. For our part, we ought to see Mexico not as an isolated fatherland, but as part of the larger context, which is Latin America. When we manage that, it will be splendid. It will make for an extraordinary cinema, one very much our own."

"Won't there be too many obstacles to achieving this objective?"

"It is a complex affair, in which many aspects come into play, like those of economics and production. Mexico is the only Latin American country which has a more or less strong industry. In Argentina, cinema has had a very disjointed evolution, and in Brazil it hasn't gone beyond a rather low level. You could say, without fear of falsifying things, that it is still a niggardly cinema. For that reason, we would perhaps have to be the initiators of this great movement."

"What orientation would the Latin American cinema have?"

"It would be identified with the liberal political movements of our countries."

"And would it be economically feasible?"

"Of course it would pay for itself. At least that."

"And wouldn't there be problems with the United States?"

"I don't think we ought to ask their permission."

"Would it necessarily have to be political?"

"From religious to a cinema which simply puts on the screen what one lives every day. In Latin America, very important things are happening and art ought to reflect them, with objectivity."

On the set of *Coronación,* another Olhovich film

"Will anybody decide to do it?"

"Yes, definitely. There is no doubt about it. Why wouldn't we generate this kind of cinema, which in some way will embrace our conflicts and hopes? We're brothers, and the proof is that no citizen of any one of our countries feels like a foreigner in the others. If I were directing in Venezuela, for example, I'd feel as comfortable and at home as in Veracruz where I was born."

The Present Latin American Cinema: Pretext to Economize

Olhovich speaks with total confidence. He has the certainty of someone who does not make mistakes. Besides, he gives me the impression of being a supremely educated man without the slightest bit of pedantry.

"I think" I say to him, "that we now have at least the beginnings of this Latin American cinema. For example, I've read in the newspapers about some of our producers who are working in Venezuela, since you mentioned that country."

"Yes, but what they've done up to now is another thing. Basically, it is negative because their only motive is to save money. What matters to these gentlemen isn't cinema. They don't take it seriously. They think about money, as if cinema were any other business. They reveal enormous disrespect for the public by not having eyes for anything but the box office."

The True Mission of the Cinema

"This is contradictory," continues Olhovich, "because the cinema is the art most tied to society these days. Because of a series of circumstances, until now it's been in the hands of the upper classes. Cinema is the affair of a minority, not of the peasants or workers, which means that the subject matter is for an elite."

"But now, with the presence of you directors, don't you think that subject matter is beginning to change?"

"There is no doubt that there is an intermediate generation,

A scene from *La casa del sur*

one of transition. Perhaps that's why they call us the new cinema. The truth is that we've broken that famous barrier and introduced focuses and themes that weren't dealt with before. This young outlook can be seen even in production and in the role that the director plays. Presently the director has responsibilities that were previously denied him. He is beginning truly to become a creator, although we're still subjects of the elite. I think the problem will end by resolving itself now that those who follow us are more conscientious and of more plebeian backgrounds."

"Then even the system will change because of those thinking up and choosing plots."

"Naturally, the cineast should be very aware of what's happening in this country. He should identify with the people in order to participate in daily life. If he understands what's happening, what affects the people, and what the people are living and breathing, he will have a chance of producing good films. There is a change of attitudes which has barely become noticeable but which has to reach full scope, so that the director or cineast in general can no longer spend his life in the studios inventing totally unrealistic stories. There is no longer room for operettic cinema, which is false and deceitful in every way."

"But don't you think that the cinema as a means of diversion is also very respectable?"

"Of course. Cinema is a two-sided art. One side is trying to achieve esthetic values, but the other intends to entertain the public. Unfortunately producers have almost exclusively taken advantage of the second form, and besides that, have not achieved the quality that the resources they use would permit. They have taken advantage of the low cultural level of the people to deceive them, as well as to enrapture them. The bad thing is that the people have fallen into the trap and become attached to the Saint and charros.

"Basically the matter is pretty simple," continues Olhovich after a brief pause. "It all consists of amusing people and in making them think at the same time. Authenticity in cinema would depend on this—something that won't be achieved in a day, and which directly depends on changes occurring in the country."

"But won't a moment come when the bad producers will outsmart themselves—that is, a time when their false cinema will make them lose money and will alienate the spectators?"

"Eventually, yes. In fact, the old impunity is disappearing because you cannot deceive the public indefinitely."

The Great Deficiencies of Our Film Industry

"All right, but we can't forget, Mr. Olhovich, that the cinema is not an art that maintains itself in a vacuum. There is also an industry; and one faces commercial problems. How do you think we can overcome these problems?"

"Our cinema is poor. We cannot compete with North American films that cost twenty million dollars. This amount exceeds by many times the largest of our budgets. Besides, it permits a filming time ten times that which is common here. On the other hand, we have to fight against a superdeveloped technique and against an industry that is totally up-to-date with regard to all kinds of innovations. We're at least a decade behind. In Mexican studios there are cameras that were built in the 1940s. Add to that the modesty of our laboratories and the low quality of sound that we give our films. After all, here is where a good excuse for many of our directors lies; and it's not artful dodging, but something that is completely based in fact. Whoever makes a film in three weeks, with these material limitations, will never be able to obtain universally appreciable quality. With all these inconveniences, we go on the market, and as is logical, fail most of the time. To technical poverty one must add, as we've seen, the penury of ideas: the outlook is very discouraging."

The Young Directors

"Apart from the changes taking place in the country, isn't there an intrinsic quality in you directors that points toward a new cinema?"

"I believe there is, although it doesn't imply special merits. Age is a determining factor. Besides that, we make up a group of friends who are in constant communication. It's not that we work as a team, but we do talk together a lot, and we're used to listening to our friends' opinions. For us it is true that several heads think better than one, and without sacrificing our author's independence. Now, for example, I'm reading a script of Jaime H. Hermosillo's, and I'm going to give him my points of view. This happens all the time among us."

"Then you think that the Mexican cinema, after all, has a promising future?"

"I think there are favorable circumstances, one of which is the logical appearance of new promotions of cineasts; another, governmental policy, which, in truth, has helped and opened doors for us."

"I say good-bye then to the director of *Muñeca reina* and *El encuentro,* a very professional cineast; a professor of cinema at CUEC "by duty and by choice"; a very stable man; and a sensible man, notwithstanding the passion that exists in all things.

12

Arturo Ripstein

"The fundamental problems, not only with Mexican cinema, but also with any other film industry, are production, distribution, exhibition, and censorship—in addition to the human element with regard to talent and knowledge of the work."

This is one of the first sentences I manage to get from Arturo Ripstein in the course of the interview. I had heard him speak many times before. We had spoken of assorted things because I had gone to the Churubusco Studios several days running. He was in full swing with the preparation of *El Santo Oficio*, hiring artists and extras. He very politely took notice of me, but did not have time to talk. Certainly these events enabled me to realize the total precision of this cineast with regard to detail. He analyzed the costumes crease by crease, compared the profile of the applicants for the parts with his notes about the characters, and managed not to leave anything to chance.

"The first problem, that of production, is clearing up for us," he adds from behind his desk. "Cinema is opening up to the new generation although there are still obstacles and other

149

irreconcilable factors. Not everyone can make films in Mexico. It continues to be a question of fortune, of luck. The directors' union is currently closed to those trying to get in."

"Yes, but the fact is that frequently films of you young directors are shown."

"True, but think of the fact that eight years ago I was the youngest director. I was twenty-one years old then. Now I'm twenty-nine, and I'm still the youngest. We're no longer spring chickens, but no one has entered the field after us."

"How many kinds of directors are there in Mexican cinema?"

"It's hard to classify them, but actually there are only two groups: the good ones and the bad ones. There is a nucleus that you could call "classical," in which there are really very few— but very important—names. Fernando de Fuentes is one of them; Alejandro Galindo is another, and of course, El Indio Fernández."

"How many generations of cineasts have there been in Mexico?"

"Very well, assuming a cineast is whoever works with cinema in any of its aspects—director, cameraman, or handyman. But if we're just talking about directors, then I'd say that in Mexico there have only been two generations. You have to remember that the Mexican cinema isn't very old; there are the founders, some of whom are still active, and then there's our generation."

After 1965, the Renovation

"When did the renovating movement in Mexican cinema begin?"

"Exactly when we arrived on the scene, around 1965. The existence of very demanding, serious, and well-informed critics brought about as a consequence, for example, the First Competition of Experimental Cinema. I don't mean that the critics were the only factor, but it's undeniable that their influence helped create a propitious atmosphere, and that in this atmosphere it was possible to convene the aforementioned competition. Recently, thanks to new production companies

A scene from *El santo oficio*

and the support of Lic. Rodolfo Echeverría, we can count on more opportunities for making the cinema we want to."

"Let's change the subject. Tell me about your films. About *El castillo de la pureza*, already out, and about *El Santo Oficio*, just begun. To tell you the truth, I haven't seen *Tiempo de morir* or *Los recuerdos del porvenir*."

"What do you want me to tell you about my films? They yield to ideas that I've carried around a long time and which, in reality, constitute my fundamental subject matter. They're themes that are repeated because each man only tells a few stories, which he can give very different forms. Jorge Luis Borges says that in literature there are only four great themes. Four things of which you can speak. I think that if there aren't four, there are fewer. Everyone always ends up telling the same thing. Or almost always the same."

"And what are the key ideas, the obsessive themes of Arturo Ripstein?"

"As much in *El castillo de la pureza* as in *El Santo Oficio,* in *Tiempo de morir* as in *Los recuerdos,* there is the same idea, which is that of intolerance. Better said, the idea of horror when confronted with intolerance."

Ripstein makes himself more comfortable in his chair. You can tell that we have gotten onto ground he likes; or if not likes, is impassioned by.

The Eternal Evil of Intolerance

We're in the cineast's studio which is in his apartment in the suburb of Condesa. In the midst of everything, there is a small group in which the voice of José de la Colina stands out. The children walk through the house and talk with Alberto and Claudio Isaac. It is a Sunday afternoon and we are all drinking ice water. We are all sleepy after eating but my interviewee is excited by the theme which just came up.

"Note that in spite of the stories being very different, intolerance is the primary motive of *El castillo* and of *El Santo Oficio* which deals, as is logical, with the Inquisition. The same thing happened with the other two films, but since you haven't seen them it would be a little more complicated to talk about them. *El castillo de la pureza* is fiction based on a real event: that of the man who locked up his family for eighteen years and didn't let anyone peep at the street in order to keep the outside world from contaminating his loved ones. I say it's fiction because José Emilio Pacheco and I elaborated on the story and didn't have the concrete details about what had actually taken place. Now we've found out that they were even more grim than our imaginary episodes. Our basic theme was intolerance, not accepting another person; and power and authority."

"How did you and Pacheco pair up?"

"Clasa Films put me in charge of the story. Dolores del Río was going to produce it, and she herself was to act in it. Then I spoke with José Emilio, of whom I've been a friend for many

A scene from *El castillo de la pureza*

years. I've written scripts for other directors but doubt that I'd get good results by myself without a good collaborator. My collaboration with Pacheco was supremely fruitful. For his part, his work has been excellent. We understand each other very well, the proof of which is that we continued together to write *El Santo Oficio.* Look: we spent six months reading books and taking notes." And with his head, he points out to me a row of some twenty-five volumes which are on the first shelf of the bookcase behind him.

"All right, how would you define intolerance?"

"I don't pretend to define it. My language is cinematic: that is, I present my ideas with images in a particular climate. I believe, speaking of *El castillo,* that the intolerance of that family's father was as much his as it was that of the world around him. It's a sickness of the world. But I repeat, it's very hard work for me to explain my films. I believe that cinema, in the moment in which it is made clear, is nullified."

"Isn't this protagonist like the one in *La Dolce Vita* who ended up killing his children and then himself?"

"I don't know. The thing is I also don't pretend to do psychology. What I like are concrete events, solitary and photographable events. I can't, for example, make myself think about the antecedents of my stories. A character is portrayed by what he says and does in the moment of the telling. This is the true cinematic underpinning."

"How long will it take to do *El Santo Oficio*?"

"Filming will be about three months, and after that will come the staging process. In total, about six months, aside from the time we've already spent. As you can see, making a film takes a lot of time, and since you really earn very little money, it's necessary to turn to supplementary jobs. For example, I occupy myself by making television commercials. They're well paid, and they amuse me a lot."

"But how is it possible that you directors, who protest against consumer society and the entrapment of contemporary man, can devote yourselves to making commercials?"

"I do them in line with my technical quality. I'm given a job and I develop it with the greatest care. That's all. Apart from that, I've already explained to you the economic reasons. We live day to day, generally a day behind."

"You talked to me about intolerance. Does that have anything to do with censorship?"

"Of course it does. They cut films according to really strange criteria. In general there isn't any criterion, as respectable as it may seem, that's capable of legitimizing any mutilation or limitation. Generally one turns to moral interests as if they constituted a decisive argument. But I believe that no one makes anyone else go to see a film. I'm free to film if I feel like it, and in the same way, the spectator is free to attend, or not to attend, the showing of my films. They demand a lot from filmmakers: that we be consistent with reality, and that we make ourselves responsible for it. On the other hand, nobody demands this from the spectator: the spectator is very important although he is a passive subject."

The Evolution of Mexican Cinema

"Mr. Ripstein, we've spoken about various things, among them changes that reality has caused in the Mexican cinema. I'd like to be more exact about that."

"Very well, we've said that there are people with distinct ways of thinking, who are forcibly giving a new aspect to our films. It's not any easy thing, because the two generations of directors which have come about in Mexico both still exist. Think, in this case, how long-lived the profession is. Directors are the people who live longest in the entire world. Griffith, older than the themes he deals with—in other words, pre-Babylonian—died in the forties. Fritz Lang is alive and Jean Renoir. Directors don't end, but new ones appear, and accumulate. But you asked about concrete changes. One could be the power that, in our time, directors have obtained. Before, a film depended on a lot of people. The producer chose the actors, the plot, the atmosphere, and everything else. Little by little the director has become more autonomous, and the film is more his work. The work is opened to the talent and skill of an individual author. But the most profound change," continues Ripstein, "is the one you see in the way of focusing on subject matter. A more genuine, authentic attitude has been adopted."

"It seems to me the same thing is happening in literature."

Ripstein makes a gesture of agreement.

The Lack of Importance of Prizes

"The work of the director must be pretty hard, isn't that true?"

"It's according to how you see it. It is the simplest thing in the world and anyone can do it. Apparently it's enough to sit down and give orders and have two or three assistants around. But to make good cinema is really the hardest thing in the world. It requires a total understanding of the work, absolute technical control, and an integral respect for the ideas and characters of the work."

"Well, you ought to feel satisfied because up to now you've

Ripstein filming *Fox Trot* on location with Charlotte Rampling, Peter O'Toole, and Max von Sydow

gotten favorable criticism, good box-office receipts, and very noteworthy prizes."

"With regard to prizes, they really don't matter much to me. At least not in their present form. Instead of little statues, I think it would be better if directors received a contract to make another film, or a cash reward. I think the international prizes are not bad—above all from the commercial point of view: they unleash very effective publicity, promote films, and ultimately get one more work."

How many other things could one talk about with Arturo Ripstein? Undoubtedly many. Almost anything cinematic, because Ripstein, like other members of his generation, is very aware of and interested in things around him. But I have to say good-bye. At the door he requests that I show him the original of my article.

"There could be mistakes and I would not like to retract what I've said." But I don't think there are any, and I'm tempted to publish these notes without this little, relative, and excusable act of censorship.

13

 **Alberto Isaac**

"What is the real problem with the national film industry?"

Alberto Isaac smiles slightly and thinks a minute.

"That is a very difficult question which has no one answer," he tells me. "Besides, one cannot say anything new, nothing that the public at hand does not already know. Also, I don't feel that I'm enough of an authority to expound this point. I'm not even slightly oracular ... It's strong enough to indicate that something is lacking—or that there is too much of something else."

"All right. But as a filmmaker, you must have thought about this matter occasionally. What do you think about it?"

"Look, I think, summing up a lot and trying to synthesize, that what our cinema lacks is looking honestly at Mexico, and reflecting it."

We are in Isaac's home, along Tacubaya. It is very early in the morning. He has invited me to breakfast and received me in a small room, full of books and miscellaneous objects, on the top floor. There is a window through which one of the trees in

161

the garden shows. Light comes into the room, and from time to time a Siamese cat, who is playing between the window sash and the tree branches, appears.

"Has the Mexican cinema never been honest?"

"Never. It's beginning to be now, at least in part. The day we can make films about the principal national problems, about corruption, bureaucracy, the PRI, Fidel Velázquez*— that day we'll be able to begin to talk about authenticity . . ."

Isaac reflects for a few moments, his eyes fixed on his plate. "Although, if we think about it, and look at other countries of the world, maybe we could arrive at the conclusion that in none of them is cinema of this type allowed. A cinema that blasts society and the state without any control. Curiously, the only cinema that has these freedoms, although they are not absolute, is that of the United States. Outside of there, I don't think there is another exception. We cannot imagine that in Cuba a film about the behavior of homosexuals would be made; or that in Czechoslovakia they'd film one about the Prague spring; or that in Hungary they would use the events of 1956 as subject matter. You ask yourself—and the answer is doubtful —if in Russia you would speak of intellectuals imprisoned in psychiatric clinics in a film. True or not? Here in our country we are asking the government to finance a film about Tlatelolco** and maybe this will push the machinery a little. Now then, if we make this film, it will be a magnificent sign. It will indicate that we've achieved a singular maturity."

"Yes, truly, a theme of that kind could be too strong, but there are things like corruption, undernourishment, neolatifundism, whose cinematographic treatment, as long as it was intelligent, could do a lot . . . But, tell me, how could you film something about Tlatelolco?"

"There have been some attempts already. There are various plots, and some things have been written . . . I find an article that José Emilio published in *Excelsior* fascinating. It deals with a young man who was born twenty years before Tlatelolco. The day of the tragedy he received a fundamental expe-

*Fidel Velázquez, head of Mexico's largest labor union, the Confederation of Mexican Workers (CTM) [*Trans. note*]

**The site of the 1968 student demonstrations which led to a bloody confrontation with the government [*Trans. note*]

rience which makes him change his whole life. This article by
José Emilio is not yet a plot, but it constitutes something like
a skeleton—a first draft that can be filled in and completed."

The History of a Cineast

I am sitting in front of Isaac, who is eating a hearty breakfast.
I have to resign myself to a grapefruit since I'm on a diet.

"I am already familiar with your previous production," I tell
him. "I remember *En este pueblo no hay ladrones* which, if
I'm not mistaken, you presented at the First Competition of
Experimental Cinema."

"Yes, that was in 1965. The plot is from Gabriel García
Márquez. And many of my friends worked on it—like Mon-
siváis, García Márquez himself, Juan Rulfo, La China Mendoza,
José Luis Cuevas, Abel Quezada . . . in short, a lot of people.
Even Luis Buñuel appears in it."

"Next came *Las visitaciones del diablo,* with a plot by
Emilio Carballido."

"Yes, that was the film that opened the door to the union for
me. The thing is, to get into that group—to the directors'
section—you have to have made a picture that took at least five
weeks to film."

"Yes. I learned of that circumstance, which I certainly think
implies a vicious circle, because in order to be a unionized
director they demand a work that they only entrust to experienced and prestigious people."

"The thing is that Ripstein and I did the apprenticeship
together. The same person opened the road for us; that is,
Ripstein's own father. He financed my *Visitaciones* and Arturo's film.

"After that, if I'm not mistaken, you made a film of the
Olympic games, then of the soccer championship, and later,
Los días del amor and *El rincón de las vírgenes.*"

"The last two I filmed in Colima, which as you know is my
home and the place I go whenever I can. I've lived here in the
capital many years, but I have not stopped feeling provincial."

While Alberto Isaac tells me this, I think that he has the
appearance of a British gentleman, a writer of political novels,

A scene from *Tívoli*. Alfonso Arau collaborated with Alberto Isaac in the making of this film, which depicts the decade of the forties in Mexico City.

or a lion hunter. Nonetheless, he is from the provinces, admits it, and acts in accordance with his origin and preferences. The thing is that he is a very active provincial person, as they all must be. He remembers that he left Colima because he swam very well, he even won national, Central American, and who knows what other kinds of championships. Here in the capital he started drawing, writing, and, of course, directing films.

"I really like working on the provincial world because it is what I know about. Nonetheless, right now I'm planning a totally Mexico City–oriented film, which will be called *Tívoli*. It will tell the story of the lives of those who work in that little theater . . . Surely you've heard of it. It will be the history of its decline under Uruchurtu.* Alfonso Arau and I collaborated on the plot and the treatment of it is completely mine."

"Up to now which of your films do you like best?"

"*Los días del amor,* which took place in Colima and is the most personal. I could even say that it's semibiographical. It seems that that is the way, at least in my case. Of course, other possibilities tempt me, like, for example, those present in the books of Rulfo. In *El rincón de las vírgenes* I used two of Juan's stories that held a great attraction for me, which I couldn't resist. It was a very difficult challenge facing me since I had to find the relation between them—in other words, between 'El día del derrumbe' and 'Anacleto Morones.' At first glance they're very different pieces and to find a connecting thread took a lot of work on my part. Certainly the central character of 'Anacleto Morones' was played by El Indio Fernández. I thought long and hard to find an actor. I even thought of Ricardo Montalbán, who perhaps would have been able to come from Hollywood. But finally I realized that Emilio Fernández was my character. I worked with him with great pleasure because he's a very good professional actor, although there was one difficulty after another. Above all, because he directs films and it is not easy to accommodate yourself to the demands of a strange individual."

The Director Takes Command

"How long do you take on a film, from the very beginning?"

"The films that are being made right now in Mexico don't correspond in the traditional sense to our earlier filmmaking. They do not follow only the demands of the industry and business. This is noticeable in everything: production time is one of these details. Five weeks is the normal time now, which represents a gain in care, craft, and technical resources."

"So that there really has been a change."

"Of course. Now the film revolves more around a single person, the director. From the conception of the plot, the

*Ernesto P. Uruchurtu, mayor of Mexico City from 1952 to 1966.

director is apt to be around, so that the work develops as a
unity and not as an aggregation of more or less unconnected
pieces. I think this policy gives good results. In my particular
case, I take part in the planning of all the details. In the choice
of clothes, in the scenery—although, as is natural, with the help
of specialists. With regard to backgrounds, my wife helps me
a lot. Now then, by acquiring more power, the directors also
acquire greater responsibility. There's a moment in which one
is alone with his film, and he has to follow and care for it. One
gets involved in the technical process, in the finish . . . I choose
to the letter what goes into the credits, I have something to do
with the publicity, I meddle in the details of launching the film,
I dispute the theaters that ought to show it . . . in short, I don't
ignore anything at all. Even when the film is being shown, I
still worry about what theater will do the second run of it; in
spite of the fact that it doesn't matter to me monetarily, I find
out how much the film made . . . As you can see, there is
another side to the director's present tasks. Hired directors,
who before predominated and are not entirely bad, are beginning to disappear."

"How does a hired director act?"

"Well, on Thursday he is given the script of a film that's
going to begin Monday. There is a set cast of characters, and
a prospectus of locations, all of which the producer has decided
upon. The director is limited to routine business; as quickly as
he can finish filming, he forgets the picture. An editor sets up
the film as he wishes, and then comes the launching in which
the director has neither art nor part. This, which in some cases
continues to happen, was the rule in Mexican cinema until just
recently. That is, these directors can have a lot of work, and be
very good craftsmen, but they're not artists. But we should not
lose sight of the fact that in our cinematography there have
always been directors of great professional integrity who have
won solid prestige. Ismael Rodríguez is one of them with his
vital and amusing, although Manichean, cinema. Alejandro
Galindo is another, with formidable films. It seems to me, after
reviewing the entire history of the Mexican cinema, that I
would go with Galindo. It is clear that there are other noteworthy figures, like El Indio Fernández and Gavaldón. But
Galindo at certain times has a social sense that is very impor-

tant, and which none of the others share. If you wish, he's like a slightly out-of-date leftist, a little old—but you cannot deny the nobility of the ideas in films like *Esquina, bajan, Campeón sin corona,* and *Una familia de tantas.*"

"Why hasn't anyone made films in which the principal character is a woman? I'm not referring to credits, but to the story and characters. I think Mexican cinema is fundamentally a man's cinema, and that women appear in it like pretty figures, but not like beings of flesh and blood, with all their complications and contradictions."

"Well, yes, you could be right. For my part, maybe I haven't done anything big with female characters because I feel a little incapable. In *Las visitaciones del diablo* I tried something like this, and in *Los días del amor* there is also a certain touch of feminine psychology embodied in the grandmother that Anita Blanch played. Or in the calm old maids . . . But, yes, I repeat, you're right: in Mexico there isn't a cinema that deals with women."

The Trap of Commercial Cinema

"Listen, how do you defend yourself against a strictly commercial cinema? How do you arrange to keep the producers at bay?"

"In my case, I defend myself in an easy way. I don't depend on cinema to make a living because I continue working on the newspaper. In the last two years I've turned down four films which without doubt would have made me good money. Doing them would have enabled me to leave journalism, and dedicate myself totally to directing."

"But then you would have renounced another very important thing . . ."

"Of course, my freedom."

"Then you don't believe that a director can avoid the economic problem by making commercial films in order to give himself the luxury of a good film every year or two?"

"Not true. There is a trap in taking that risk. When one gets into commercial cinema, he gets stuck, and it is very hard to regain authenticity. There are many Mexican directors who began that way, with certain purity, and later prostituted themselves. They end up as hired directors, which, as I told you, in other ways seems valid to me. I don't have any antipathy toward them; simply, my plans don't coincide with theirs."

The Troubled Road of Finances

"What do directors do to get financing for a film?"

"This is where the trouble begins, although presently we have two choices. One, we can apply to an established producer, one of the traditional ones of Mexican cinema: propose the film to him and if he accepts, well and good. On the other hand, it is possible to go to Churubusco Studios so that the producer may be the state."

"But doesn't this represent a compromise?"

"Curiously, no. The state offers more freedoms for the production of films than do private producers. Right now I'm thinking of at least three persons who, like me, have made films at Churubusco. Neither the Bank nor the Studios tries to intervene with the script. As is natural, there is prior approval of the project, and there are cases in which, after reading a script, it's rejected. But this doesn't happen more in the state circle. This happens with other producers too. The good thing about Churubusco is that when the script is given the go-ahead, the director is totally free. If the budget is accepted, he has complete facilities to cast his film and give it the finish he wants. I assure you that with no private producer do these advantages occur. It is a very old practice of our producers to use pressure so the director includes such and such a star in the films because 'she's a good box-office attraction,' or because 'he is a very good friend of mine.' In short, for them this is a business, and they have a particular idea of what ought to be done."

"But aren't there producers who have a patronlike spirit—or who have realized that good films are the ones they leave alone the most?"

"There have been but they have been burned so badly that it is impossible to gain ongoing support for these theories from them."

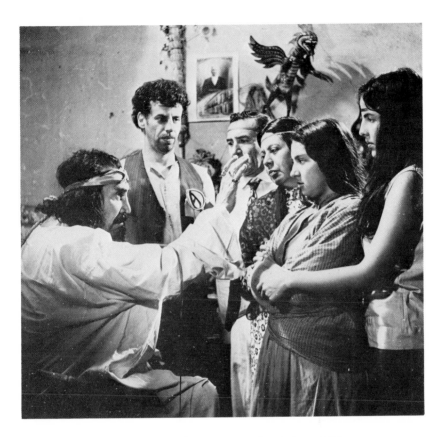

A scene from *El rincón de las vírgenes,* with Emilio Fernández and Alfonso
Arau

"Nonetheless, there is another circumstance, to my way of
thinking. And that is that a film doesn't have to be expensive
to have appreciable quality."

"Of course. The main ingredient in all films is talent. This
money point is a very common fallacy which the directors of
the old school never tire of repeating. 'If they gave me the ten
million that Cazals had to film *El jardín de tía Isabel . . .*' these
men say. They also claim that something else would happen if
instead of two weeks they had fifteen for filming. In reality, as
I told you, there is a fallacy in these wishes. Given the themes
they film, and their systems and criteria, the only thing that
would happen is that they would have nine million and ten
weeks left over. They're used to making a set product, and
outside influences—like time and money—would not change
the results at all."

The Possibilities of the New Cinema

Isaac has now finished his breakfast, before my envious eyes, and he tells me quickly about the troubles he has to put up with currently so that a film has the correct finish from the technical point of view.

"It's that the union," he affirms, "has abused its function. They don't stop with protecting their workers, but they protect mediocrity. There have been cases in which a film, by some sort of negligence, comes out with a flaw. As is natural, the director or producer complains about the lack of care, but the union contents itself with a friendly twinking of the ears of the person responsible, without applying any sanction."

"Changing the subject—what effects did the First Contest of Experimental Cinema have?"

"I think that apart from the films that it made known, there were other intangible, but possibly more important, effects. That contest made it so that in Mexico we are aware that a different cinema could be made, and also that it was necessary to try to do it. The young people and the public were excited by this perspective, which isn't illusory. To show that it isn't, there were the films I told you about."

"Well, I think that the Mexican cinema, with the new generation's talent, with the loosening up of the authorities, with the pressure from the critics, and with the evolution of the audience, has a wide road ahead of it."

"I agree with you. Above all, with respect to the subjects our cinema can treat, there is no doubt that the future is very promising. It happened that I was chosen to go to Chile with President Echeverría in 1972, and in that country he made very promising statements. He spoke about the mission of the cinema, as a means of waking the popular conscience to the most important problems around us, and of the duty of the cineast to make films of this sort; to forget about the others that neither say nor communicate anything. He opened up encouraging vistas to us."

Selected Readings

Ayala Blanco, Jorge. *La aventura del cine mexicano.* Mexico City: Ediciones Era, 1968.

Burns, E. Bradford. *Latin American Cinema: Film and History.* Los Angeles: UCLA Latin American Center, 1975.

Galindo, Alejandro. *Una radiografía histórica del cine mexicano.* Mexico City: Fondo de Cultura Popular, 1968.

García Riera, Emilio. *Medio siglo de cine mexicano.* Mexico City: U.N.A.M., 1960.

Index

173